THE DRAGON RALLY

By C. A. Morgan

ACKNOWLEDGEMENTS

I wish to thank the many people who have helped me put this book together. With special thanks to the Conwy M.C.C, especially Ken Davies, Morton Media, other Motorcycle Magazines, and of course all the Dragon Rallyists who have contributed their own stories to be included in the book.
I cannot forget my family either who without the help of my husband's scrapbook on The Dragon Rally, this book would not of been put together.
I have tried to put as much information as was available to me to make this book complete. I hope you enjoy this book.

This book is dedicated to 'Bomber' Thomas, all the other members of the Conwy M.C.C, and all the Dragon Rallyists, past and present.

Bryn 'Bomber' Thomas-sadly passed away in Oct 2008-pictured here with his wife Glenys Thomas-1991 Riverside, Capel Curig, Dragon Rally.

ISBN 978-0-9575984-0-9

Rod Morgan, Frank Rodway and Ken Short with the Dragon Rally Mascot at the 1997 Dragon.

Second Edition 2013

Front cover photograph :- Taken outside The White Lion, getting ready to head off to the Dragon Rally 1966. Riders from left to right, Tom Jones, Mike Bone, Brian Wynn, Fred Bayliss, Bernie Pierce, Ralph Jones, Selwyn Richards, Bob White, Steve Griffiths, Colin Roberts and Angie Blackwell.

Published by MorganMaps©

Contents

DRAGON RALLY VENUES

YEAR	RALLY SITE	WEATHER (If Known)
1962	Bryn Bras Castle near Llanrug	Cold, dry, snow
1963	Gwrych Castle, Abergele	Cold with snow
1964	Gwrych Castle, Abergele	Warm, sunny
1965	Ex R.A.F. Camp, Glyn Padarn Llanberis	Cold, showery
1966	Ex R.A.F. Camp, Glyn Padarn Llanberis	Rain, floods
1967	Tyddyn- Rhonwy, Llanberis	Warm, sunny
1968	Tyddyn- Rhonwy, Llanberis	Rain
1969	Tyddyn- Rhonwy, Llanberis	Snow
1970	Tyddyn- Rhonwy, Llanberis	
1971	Glyn Padarn, Llanberis,(Dragon Rally Club split)	Cold, wet, icy
1972	Ex R.A.F. Camp, Llanberis (last one here)	Cold, dry
1973	Dewi Gofer Scramble Course	
1974	Tyn-y-Berth, off A470 Betws-y-Coed	Cold, muddy, 'Somme Rally'
1975	Riverside, Capel Curig	Dry, cold
1976	Riverside, Capel Curig	Cold,wet,snowy
1977	Garth Farm, Twin Lakes, Capel Curig	Cold, Snowy
1978	Plas Irwg, Llanrwst	
1979	Plas Irwg, Llanrwst	
1980	Bryn Gloch, Betws Garmon	Wet, muddy
1981	Riverside, Capel Curig	Cold, dry
1982	Riverside, Capel Curig	Dry, cold
1983	Riverside, Capel Curig	Mild, dry, misty
1984	Pant-y-Cyff, Pentir near Bangor	Cold
1985	Gwrych Castle, Abergele	Fantastic snow!
1986	Riverside, Capel Curig	Cold, dry
1987	Riverside, Capel Curig	Cold, damp
1988	Nant-Gwynant, Beddgelert	Rain,mud,floods

DRAGON RALLY VENUES

YEAR	RALLY SITE	WEATHER (If Known)
1989	Riverside, Capel Curig	Rain
1990	Riverside, Capel Curig	Rain, Snow
1991	Riverside, Capel Curig	Snow
1992	Riverside, Capel Curig	Dry, warm
1993	Riverside, Capel Curig	Dry,warm,sunny
1994	Garth Farm, Twin Lakes, Capel Curig	Warm, sunny
1995	Riverside, Capel Curig	Wet all day!
1996	Voryd Bay nr Caernarvon Airport	Wet Sat,Dry Sun
1997	Riverside, Capel Curig	Dry
1998	Riverside, Capel Curig	Dry, windy
1999	Riverside, Capel Curig	
2000	Riverside, Capel Curig	Windy, wet
2001	Voryd Bay nr Caernarvon Airport	Wet and muddy
2002	Caernarvon Airport	Dry, sunny
2003	Caernarvon Airport	Windy but dry
2004	Riverside, Capel Curig	Wet and windy
2005	Pentrefoelas, Glasfryn	Cold
2006	Ty-Croes, Trac Mon, Anglesey	Dry but cold
2007	Anglesey Showground	Dry but cold
2008	Cae Du, Beddgelert	Dry, warm
2009	Ty-Croes, Trac Mon, Anglesey	Cold, snowy
2010	Glyn Bach, near Rowen	Dry, frosty
2011	Sygun, Near Beddgelert. 50th Dragon Rally	Cold, dry, then wet & windy

This list was mainly compiled by Bomber -Bryn Thomas- of the Conwy M.C.C.

MAP OF DRAGON RALLY SITES

THE DAWN OF THE DRAGON

The Dragon Rally found it's roots in North Wales with the Conwy M.C.C, after many motorcycle enthusiasts called for something similar in Britain, to the Elephant Rally, held in Nurburgring in Germany during January.
February was the chosen month, and most of them have been held in the second week of February to give everyone a couple of weeks to warm up after the deep snows of the Elephant Rally.

John Ebbrell was one of the scouts searching for a perfect location with the help of Conwy Club Chairman Don Williams. After much searching the first Dragon was held at Bryn Bras Castle in 1962, with the first 'Dragon badge' been a fabric hand embroidered patch, of which only 1,200 were made And over 2000 riders attended the first Dragon Rally. Rallyists had the choice of paying 2s. 6d to receive one of the sow on patches, which are now highly sort over by Dragon Rally enthusiasts and collectors.

The Dragon then moved to Gwrych Castle, near Abergele, for the next couple of years, but by 1965 a bigger venue was needed. So it then moved to the Ex R.A.F camp near Llanberis, which is now a Business park, but was know to most as Glyn Padarn. And was where the famous headlight parade was held. The numbers continued to grow and were soon exceeding 5000. Which in itself caused a few problems locally, within the public houses and community. It was becoming so popular that it was beginning to start rifts in the Conwy club.

In 1968 '*The Motor Cycle'* produced the first paper sticker which was purple with yellow writing and white adhesive (that stuck well on to anything apparantly!) But it was not the first official sticker made by the Conwy M.C.C.

But however in 1969 heavy snow caused numbers to drop drastically, mainly due to people not been able to get to the rally, and it is rumoured that many of the badges were sacrificed to the lake.

JOHN EBBRELL IN SNOWDONIA IN SEARCH OF AN ELEPHANT AND FINDS A DRAGON

As I drank up my coffee, I watched the sunset fade behind the distant mountains. " I've got a special job for you", Harry Louis had told me. Motor cyclists all over the country are demanding a British Elephant Rally- and they want it soon. Go to North Wales on a recce for a place to hold it."

Here without doubt, was the ideal area. Wales is a respectable run from Birmingham and the industrial North, yet within a weekend's reach of hard riders anywhere. Less than five hours out from London I was already in the hills. And before I was to leave I had found the ideal spot. Bryn Bras Castle, right at the foot of Snowdon. Remember the name: Bryn Bras.

Here was no empty shell, but an hotel and restaurant as well as a castle. Conwy Club chairman Don Williams and I discovered large, well furnished rooms with fireplaces in baronial style, set about a maze of passages and stairs. It would be just the thing for the friendly get-togethers motor cyclists love; plenty of room for hundreds of riders, yet cosy enough for the smallest party.

There was light, warmth, somewhere for a wash and to leave riding kit. A barbecue or buffet supper could be arranged for any number. No shortage of parking space in the grounds either. A few of the crowd-perhaps 80- could stay overnight in the castle proper. Camping facilities were available too. The management would welcome the rally at Bryn Bras. We could rent the whole place, make it our own for one night.

But back to the story that led to the discovery. All the way up that splendid hard-in-third-gear climb out of Llangollen, the Leaders headlamp turned each cat's eye into tiny lighthouses. A5 is the gateway to North Wales. In whichever place the rally was held, the bulk of the riders would travel this road, climbing the moors after Corwen, winding up the grip along the two-mile straight from Cerrigydruidion. The luck of a clear day would give them a tantalizing glimpse of Snowdon itself before they dived down the tree-lined bends into Betws-y-Coed.

Is there a Leverkus in Caernarvonshire? indeed there is nearly 50 of them-for the Conwy Club invited me to discuss the rally with them. Their Clubroom in the shadow of the famous castle, was crowded that night, for though the club is modest in membership figures, there is no lack of enthusiasm. Like thousands of other motor cyclists their imaginations had been fired by George Wilsons call for an Elephant Rally in Britain. There were riders here tonight from all over North-west Wales; they knew the district; they had contacts. When did they want the Rally? February. How soon did they want it to start? Now! We quickly got to work. However tough rally riders might be, they would demand certain facilities-a roof over their heads, a hot meal, a warm fire, a place to clean themselves up, somewhere to spend the night. The last problem was easily solved. Everywhere in North Wales there are hotels, inexpensive guest-houses and farms, and camping sites for the hard men.

IT would simply be a matter for the organizers to collect addresses within a ten-mile radius of the meeting place.
That was going to be the ticklish point. Wales has nothing to equal the Nurburgring in Germany, with its assembly hall, restaurant and all the rest. Somebody suggested a hotel. But where could one big enough be found? The Nurburgring attracts 1,000 riders. Besides, Who was going to ride 300 miles just to go to an hotel? Something more dramatic, more in the spirit of the thing, was demanded.

A castle would be the very place! Wales was full of them. So we must find one with at least the minimum mod.cons. Their home-town castle was therefore out of the picture, but the Conwy boys told me that 15 miles along the coast, close to Bangor, stood Penrhyn Castle. It had been built by a 19th -century millionaire: now it was in the hands of the National Trust.

So two days later, Don Williams and I took the magnificent *corniche* road to Bangor. Penrhyn Castle was palatial beyond description. We went in to meet the National Trust authorities. But it was a no go. An "Elephant" would be too unconventional for them. " Next year perhaps," was the nearest we got.

Why not Glynllifon, south of Caernarvon? suggested the information office in Bangor. This turned out to be a mansion owned by the County Education Authority, for residential Courses. Set in parkland it looked attractive enough through binoculars, but a check at the county offices closed the matter. There was no accommodation for large parties.

"Nitor," had thought an airfield would make a grand setting. So I had a look round the old R.A.F. Station at Llandwrog. Set on a sand-pit at the bottom of the Menai Strait and swept by a howling gale it seemed like the end of the earth. The runways stretched gaunt and deserted; the buildings were mere shells carpeted with cow dung. Nothing here for us.

It was the same story at Penrhos airfield, below Pwllheli. Well into the Lleyn now, that Peninsula which stretches into the Irish sea, I carried on through Abersoch to Hells Mouth. During the war an airfield had been built on what the Welsh call a *morfa*, or salt marsh, but today only crumbling air-raid shelters remain.

My guide book referred to a mansion at the other end of the bay, called Plas-yn-Rhiw.

10515. - CAPEL CURIG & SNOWDON

PLAS in welsh can mean a palace, but this was only a quaint little country house perched high on the tree-clad hillside. Three elderly sisters live there now. They made me a cup of tea and showed me a turret staircase in the oldest part of the house built, they said, by Prince Meirion Goch who came to win back his lands from the Vikings, 1,000 years ago. Far below, the white surf crawled in the aptly-named Hell's Mouth. What a pity the place was too small!

Back in Conwy, the clubs committee and I started a process of elimination. Anglesey was out altogether. Stately homes were non-existent and the service airfields were all in some sort of use. A call to Butlins at London soon scrubbed the possibility of their Pwllheli holiday camp- unless someone presented us with the £3,000 needed to open it!

The Ministry of works Cardiff headquarters seemed sympathetic when we approached them, but the castles in their charge-Beaumaris, Caernarvon, Criccieth were as devoid of facilities as Conwy. Harlech, the most promising of the bunch, would be closed for off-season repairs.

Next morning I set off to do the rounds of the climber's Inns in Snowdonia, (They should be used to large parties of young, jolly men.) That day the rain came down in torrents and it blew a howling gale. The welcomes I received were, I am sorry to say, scarcely more encouraging. "People come here for peace and quiet," the proprietress of one place told me. "Writers and artists stay with us in the winter. They couldn't do with the noise of all your motor bikes." I started up the Leader and squelched off down to Caernarvon. I had heard of a public hall there, called the Pavilion.

The Pavilion turned out to be nothing but a tumbledown tin shack. Nursing a cup of tea in a nearby cafe I browsed through the town guide. *Bryn Bras Castle,* the advertisement read, *offers you a welcome.....*

I discovered Bryn Bras, five miles east of Caernarvon, just off the Llanberis Pass road. The turrets and battlements glimpsed above tree tops gave it a mystery and romance of a Castle of Fairyland. Could this, at last, be the place? Yes, I say.

When I set off back to London I went round by Bryn Bras, and at the top of the hill behind the castle anchored up. In my minds eye I saw the towers floodlit, the place thronged with riders from all corners of the Kingdom, the same nocturnal cavalcade down the Llanberis pass that reader D. R. Shackles had envisaged a fortnight ago.

On this same hill the celebration bonfire would be seen winking and glowing below the snow-capped mountains, a signal that these men had come to this distant spot to pay homage to the greatest game in the world.

I thought too, of the enthusiasm of the Conwy Club, their willingness to play host to this memorable event. They were eager to be at work, translating vision into reality; to go into the details to see whether a February date could be arranged. Already they had their own name for it, the proud symbol of a proud people- The Dragon Rally.

North Wales it must be!

Written by John Ebbrell Courtesy of 'The Motor Cycle'

TARGET-THE DRAGON

Early next Saturday morning, 1,700 motorcyclists will be astir. All over Britain eager eyes will be surveying the weather, busy hands filling vacuum flasks and stowing bundles of blankets on luggage grids. Even as the bleak winter dawn is breaking hundreds of riders will have begun their long pilgrimage, with many miles behind them.

And a thousand more will sniff the morning air and wish that, they too, were on the same errand.

What is the target on which all these riders will converge? it is Bryn Bras Castle, at the foot of Snowdon, where the scene is set for the biggest ever winter gathering of dyed in-the-waders enthusiasts ever held in Britain-the Dragon Rally.

Riders will find few comforts there. Beds are available for only a handful. For the rest there will be spartan luxury of a bare floor in a barn or a marquee.There'll be cold water to wash in and though there'll be plenty to eat you'll balance your plate on your knees.

But these men have not thronged to this remote corner of Wales to lie in luxury. Nor are they here to have their palates titivated by an elaborate programme of entertainments, for they are Corinthians of the greatest game in the world.

They were inspired by an article in our own pages last autumn calling for this mighty demonstration of the brotherhood of motorcyclists. Their hosts are the lads of the Conwy Club, few in number but enthusiastic enough to turn the initial dream into magnificent reality.

However stark the comforts this weekend at Bryn Bras, rallyist will get the warmest welcome anywhere in these islands. You'll meet kindred spirits from Northern Ireland , Cornwall, Kent, faraway Ross-shire and all points in between.

There will be the pick of Britain's Motor cycles to admire' and their owners to yarn with until the we small hours. Household names in British motorcycling will rub shoulders at the castle. One of them is sidecar ace Chris Vincent, who'll be helping Barry Ryerson to run a recruiting stand for the nation-wide corps of mercy riders. And where could they find better than at the Dragon Rally?

Around a dozen German boys are coming too, veterans of their own great Elephant Rally. One king-size enthusiast on a pint-size mount is Ulnch Schwab, riding all the way from Stuttgart on a 50 cc Kreidler.

At 7.00pm Stan Alman of the Conwy Club will swing out of the castle gate to lead the spectacular climax- the headlight parade. Southward up the old mountain road will go the cavalcade, and the thrum of a thousand and more exhausts will echo over Llyn Padarn. Then back down the valley riders will return to Bryn Bras.

The moving circle of light and the glow of the welcoming bonfire will be symbols for all to see. This is the bond which links fellow riders, the beacon fire which had drawn us to the wonderful world that only true motorcycle enthusiasts can know.

From 'The Motor Cycle' Courtesy of Jan Heiland

BRYN BRAS HAS ELASTIC SIDES!

Remember what happened to Jack? He planted a bean, the story goes, and in no time at all he had not a shoot, not a sapling, but a beanstalk that disappeared into the clouds. The same sort of thing is happening with the Dragon Rally. It all began as a sort of might-be-realised dream. The Conwy Club said they would lay on the organisation. John Ebbrell tootled off to search Snowdonia for a venue and stumbled on Bryn Bras Castle which, it seemed would hold 500.

But Bryn Bras properties which put it on a plane almost with the castle in which the "fe-fi-fo-fum" giant lived at the upper end of Jack's beanstalk. For one thing it is proving to have sides made not from stone and mortar but from elastic. For the figure that could be accommodated went up to 1,000. And now it has soared again, this time to 1,300.

Actually, I'm pulling the long bow just a shade. All those bodies won't be housed under the castle grounds. Others will be in a marquee. A few toughies may decide to take their own tents.

And the 300 for whom room has been found since last week? They will go into a huge barn, whose amenities are stark and fully in the tradition on which the rally has been founded. There is a roof. There is a concrete floor. There is nothing else.

We are going to Bryn Bras as a gesture. We're going there to offer poojah at the shrine of the greatest game on earth; to show the world at large the stuff of which true motor cyclists are made; and we aren't giving a hang about what sort of winter weather we may find on the way, or about the sort of amenities-or lack of amenities- we find at Bryn Bras once the clan-gathering is under way.

In view of the challenge which the rally, by its nature, presents the response has been fantastic. Lightweight owners have done a Cronin on the Wilson proposal that the affair be limited to riders of big models.

Such has been their outcry that the Conwy Club first reduced the capacity limit from 500 c.c. to 200 c.c. and have since decided that there will be no capacity limit at all. That doesn't mean, by a very long chalk, that every enthusiast who filled in the form we published last Thursday, or completes the opposite, will be assured of a share in the adventurous weekend. When the number of forms received tops 1,300 a halt will be called-as it must if chaos is to be avoided. And that far more will want to go to Bryn Bras than can be accommodated is already evident. In spite of the Post Office work-to-rule, 650 completed forms were with the Conwy Club by last Monday Morning! The total number of beds, remember is 65. If you want to bag one of them you are asked to try to book it direct with the castle staff. BUT DO IT NOW!!

Dragon Rally

NAME..

ADDRESS..

MACHINE..

Cut this form out and post it, together with a postal order value 5s (10s if you will have a pillion or sidecar passenger) and a STAMPED ADDRESSED ENVELOPE to this address:

L. M. Irving, Milford House, Lloyd Street, Llandudno, North Wales

Your postal order should be made payable to the Conway and D.M.C.C.

The receipted form will be returned to you, and in this way will serve as your parking ticket at Bryn Bras Castle.

TAKE IT WITH YOU!

By George Wilson

THE CLAN WILL FORGATHER

As I said last week the Dragon Rally is on. It is on for one purpose- to pay homage to the great pastime of motor cycling. The dates are February 24 and 25. The venue is Bryn Bras Castle, a turreted pile nestling in Snowdon's shadow. Bryn Bras at this time of year is as good as shut up. When opened specially for the rally of the sort envisaged it will far from provide the comforts of home.

The set-up roughly is this. Some 50 or so rallyists will sleep in beds. The remainder? They will want their own bedding and they will kip down where they can. Some will sleep on the dining room floor. For others there will be the stark comfort of the floors of adjoining rooms, of the entrance hall, of cottages in the expansive grounds. For more still there will be a marquee. I reckon that by pressing all the facilities into service Bryn Bras can accommodate, in all, about 500 souls.

There will be all the camping accommodation you may want, and beds may be found for the less-rugged of the castle overflow in Caernarvon. But the top limit will be 1,000, and for that reason the Conwy Club is restricting the gathering to over 200 c.c. models.

It'll probably have to be a case of first come first served. Those who arrive early can bag their bed space by dumping their riding gear on it. Those who arrive after that had better bring tents or be prepared to spend the night standing up. But since only the enthusiasts of the true genre will be there anyway, they won't mind that. They can use the hours to yarn about the subject closest to their hearts, and what better way of spending a night than that?

Imagine this courtyard at Bryn Bras Castle thronged with riders from every corner of the British Isles

What will that sort of cold comfort cost? It'll go something like this; if you get a bed the price for that luxury together with dinner, breakfast and lunch will be £2.2s; if you kip down on the floor (one pace forward all you old sweats) the price will be £1.1s.

In the way of organised entertainment there won't be much. There will be a barbecue in the summer house in the grounds on the Saturday night; there will be a film show; there will be a bonfire outside the summer house. Maybe the Conwy Club lads, who are laying on the rally, will organise the sort of massed ride which is such a feature of the German Elephant Rally on which the Dragon is based.

As to other facilities I can tell you now that if you won't be prepared to queue up for access to a wash basin, then the Dragon is not for you. Petty inconveniences there will be, and those by the score. But the Conwy Club isn't laying on this great weekend for petulant children.

It is laying it on for men-and girls and women, too-for whom all the barriers in the world wouldn't be big enough or strong enough to keep them away.

Snowdonia is tranquil at this time of year. The hotels and boarding houses are empty and the local larder holds just enough food for the populace. For that reason the Conwy Club is asking every enthusiasts who intends- and no messing-to be there to complete the form at the end of this article. It is a means of getting the quartermaster to order enough food and drink and yet not grossly over-order. Only if every seriously intentioned rallyist completes the form and sends it off will the success of the rally be assured.

As to the deposit. As the form states that it is merely a machine levy to cover organising costs. But forget to bring your receipted form with you and you will have to fork out again at Bryn Bras.

If you are only half enthusiastic about attending, if you feel that rain, wind, snow and ice are likely to deter you then forget the whole thing, for in that case this really is not for you.

The Dragon Rally is to be a clan gathering and the clan will admit to its brotherhood no man or woman who can be beaten by the elements on two wheels or three. There will be no prizes for arriving from the other end of the earth, no souvenirs, nothing that will prove to other wayfarers that you may have done something out of the ordinary.

For the sort of clan that will raise its standard at Bryn Bras has need of none of these things. Its standard will be as noble as any other in the whole wide world but it will be intangible- woven from the spirit of hardihood and brotherhood rather than from fabric and cotton.

No matter who you are in the world of motor cycling you will never be invited. You go of your own free will and at your own expense or not at all. The very essence of the whole thing, in fact, is that everyone who goes wants above all else to do so. It is for that reason that the gathering is to be staged in mid-winter and in non luxury conditions.

Probably I have said enough for the time being. But before ending I would repeat this: if you are a really seriously determined Dragonist, if you are prepared to tackle hell and high water to qualify for membership of the Clan Dragon, fill in and dispatch your form today.

By George Wilson courtesy of 'The Motor Cycle'

THE DAY OF THE DRAGON 1962

All Saturday riders poured into Snowdonia. From every corner of these islands they came, converging on the A5, Telford's great highway to the west. They raised their hands in salute as they passed, for the badge of the Dragon man was a bedroll lashed to the carrier. The spirit became infectious and children ran to the cottage gates to wave.

Seemingly endless, the cavalcade climbed through pine forests beyond Betws-y-Coed, every man-jack eager for a close-up of the real mountains. There was a following wind, sharp edged as a razor. Snowdon's triple peaks were flecked with snow, her torrents frozen to the miniature glaciers. As they swung past the slate green waves of Llyn Padarn beyond Llanberis, riders rose on their footrests. And there they had their first glimpse of Bryn Bras Castle. They saw a fairytale outline, nestling mid'trees. For most it had been an inspiring journey, with nothing to complain of but the cold. Not so for two sidecar outfits from Darlington. Over the short cut through Ruithin the B.S.A.'s chain broke and jammed immovably round the gear-box sprocket. They hitched a tow with the other outfit- a Brough Superior- and the grand old vee-twin did its best until, within spitting distance of the top of the Llanberis Pass, the rear cylinder dried up. So in Dragon Rally spirit the outfits were manhandled over the hump and coasted down the other side.

Bryn Bras castle in all its glory

Then there was the farthest-travelled of all, 56-year-old Paul Heidiger from Switzerland. Not long after leaving home he took a tumble on ice on his B.M.W, putting the headlamp out of commission. But he carried on undaunted.

As Saturday afternoon merged into evening the lineup of machines became more and more impressive. Interesting, in the view of the controversy that raged over capacity limitations,was the fact that the over whelming majority were bigsters ,with a very large proportion of sidecars.

As the light faded from the winter sky the tempo at the castle speeded. Machines moved into formation for the headlight parade. then suddenly, the mutter of engines rose to a crescendo. Out of the trees emerged a succession of headlights, their beams swathing into the darkness, a column of light, snaking up the mountain side. Far away, towards Llanberis, went the dot-dot-dot of pin-pointed rear lamps: an endless chain of light five miles long. That was an unforgettable display.

The Parade over, the vast celebration bonfire in the castle paddock blazed triumphantly. And on the other side of the castle, everyone gathered to hear the address of welcome from Conwy Club Chairman Don Williams. Harry Louis said a few words. And then came the evening's most inspiring moments

THE DAY OF THE DRAGON 1962

"To your great Dragon Rally in the country of the Red Dragon, I send the hearty wishes of the Elephant Men. My dear friends, we need real men who will face hardships to keep alive the real spirit of the true motor cyclist, to set right all the troubles in our world." That was the recorded voice of Ernst Leverkus, father of the German Rally- and indirectly of the Dragon Rally.

A convoy of rally goers brave the snow on route to the first event at Bryn Bras Castle in 1962. Bikes with fairings and chairs attached are the obvious choice in this sort of weather.

From the loudspeakers then came the stirring strains of an old sea-shanty, the song of the Elephant Men. There came the sound of racing exhausts. Inspiration was complete.

Nine members of the Motor Cycle staff had ridden to the Dragon. To them, from every hand, came thanks for the rally idea.

Yes here at Bryn Bras was the dedicated Motor cyclist, and he was been steeped in an atmosphere which could do no more than make him a greater dedicate still.

Here, by the hundred, was the sort of enthusiast who typified the spirit of the mercy riders and the proposed fellowship.

Proposed Fellowship? Here was proof of a fellowship as old and as firm as the great pastime of motorcycling itself.

Take the lad over there, waving a barbecued chicken leg to make a point he's arguing.

A lone wolf Triumph rider from Norwich, he'll sleep tonight fully dressed in a two-man tent with three enthusiasts he had never set eyes on till an hour or two earlier. Tomorrow he'll fight his way back to East Anglia. Through blinding snowstorms and over miles of ice-bound roads. Why did he come to the Dragon Rally? Let's stroll over and ask. He turns from his friends and replies: " Because I count myself a real motor cyclist. I need not say no more.

Courtesy of The 'Motor Cycle'

DRAGON MAGIC WEEKEND

Well, what was it about the Dragon Rally that made it such an incredibly outstanding success? To that question there is probably no clear-cut answer. For me it was the weekend of a lifetime for reasons too complex to enumerate, too tangible to express in mere words. But let's have a try. The rally for me was successful from a moment that will live with me always. I was nipping smartly up the A5 with a superb new A650 Star B.S.A. and Watsonian Monza when, momentarily baulked by traffic, I was overtaken by two soloists. Both riders were young. Both were bone domed. Both rode sixty-five twins and both models were burnished. In that winter sunshine they gleamed as though they had come straight off the Earls Court floor. These solos led me for a spell, cruising in the lower sixties and the skill with which they were being used took the breath away. When the time came for me to overtake there came courteous waves-on and a friendly thumbs-up sign. Wherever other enthusiasts were encountered, paused at the roadside or on the move, that thumbs-up was repeated. And so, as if by that simple yet so mystical process, the great cavalcade was welded into a vast, tight-knit family long before Bryn Bras was reached. At the castle the welding process continued. You could feel the matiness, the camaraderie- call it what you will- charging the very air we breathed. Everyone was a friend, you felt, who'd be prepared to keep his shoulder alongside yours against any odds. And if the run to Snowdonia and that Saturday night at Bryn Bras were charged with magic so was the return run on Sunday. Greeting signs by then came as a matter of course. And at the end of it all? Was this great family dispersed, broken up, swept away like snowflakes before that Sunday gale? Far from that. It is my belief that from the Dragon Rally there has emerged afresh the knowledge that all motor cyclists are brothers in fact. The magic of that wintry weekend swept high over the castle ramparts, high over Snowdon's snow-capped pate to every corner of these islands- and even to the continent too. The Dragon Rally gave expression to the entire motor cycle movement.

The greatest single contribution to the rally came, of course from the Conwy clubmen. But the palm for the runner-up performance goes, probably, to the Oxfordshire and District Sidecar Club. Two readers, wrote about the Dragon, and mention the hospitality received on the A40 at Oxford. Here is the full story. On his way to work on the Saturday morning Jack Gibbs, the clubs chairman, met two rallyisits at the roadside. He stopped to see whether help was needed, only to find that all was well, the lads were merely blowing on their hands. That simple incident triggered off a chain of events. Jack got in touch with secretary Tiny Tanner and the plans were laid. A brazier was scrounged. Some 60 miles were covered in search of necessary supplies. A board was prepared which read "Dragon Tea-up". A telephone call was put through to Bryn Bras and a message relayed over the public address that things were laid on. The brazier and supplies were transported to the chosen spot and the operation began-with what success something like 100 rallyists will vouch. Shop was opened up at 3.30pm on Sunday and the kettle was kept on the boil until seven O'clock. And that fire! it was one of those red , glowing, warm to the bone fires, and was definitely appreciated by the cold, weary rallyists.

A NEW LAIR FOR THE DRAGON

Take a good look! this is it-next winters target for every double-dyed enthusiast who calls himself a real motor cyclist. Here is Gwrych Castle, North Wales, venue-to-be of the 1963 Dragon Rally.

Gwrych (pronounce it Gree-ich) stands on the coast six miles from Rhyl, 12 miles from Llandudno. Riders along the A55 glimpse its fairytale battlements and towers against a background of wooded hills.

The place has everything Bryn Bras has and more. Boundary walls enclose 300 acres of parkland. Camping space is absolutely unlimited; you could lose the hundreds who roughed it at Bryn Bras in one corner of Gwrych.

Battlemented and turreted, the Castle is the most fantastic place ever. Flanked by ramparts and barbicans, the building stretches for nearly quarter of a mile along the hillside. Its broad terraces make the perfect setting for the super get-together. Completed in 1815, the Castle's interior has all the opulence and splendour of the regency period; oak panelling, stained glass, a grand staircase of Italian marble. Nearly 600 people can sleep here, 2,000 could find shelter if the rain came down.

Although the Castle itself may be comparatively recent, the site is famous in Welsh history, Dragon Rallyists will approach by the defile of Cefn yr Ogof, where three times the native princes of Wales threw back invading English armies with great slaughter. Here stood Shakespeare's “Barkloughly Castle,” where Richard II was betrayed to the usurping Bolingbroke. In Cae Gerail the Field of Corpses, will burn our great bonfire, a living symbol of fellowship which binds the motor cyclists of all nations.

Gwrych Castle, then, is the scene; the stage is set in early February. Organisation will, of course be in the hands of those greathearted enthusiasts, the boys of Conwy Club.

Only one thing it lacks, do you say? A mountain crossing in mid-winter. Just wait and see! You'd be surprised if you knew what is in store for the Dragon Men of 63! And as far as comfort goes, that castle will be colder than charity- that we positively guarantee.

Gwrych Castle, venue for the 1963 Dragon Rally

'WHEN THE WINDS SINGING'

The famous headlight parade of which this was taken in 1964 but it also occurred in 1963. There were sufficient machines to create a seven mile long serpent of light.

What do you think of the Dragon Rally? Not much? Then you weren't at Gwrych Castle last weekend! From Glasgow, from London, from Mancester, from Edinburgh: from all over the country they came- and 30 from Germany, too! On big bikes, on little bikes, on sidecar outfits, they filled the mountain roads from dawn till dusk.

Only two days earlier, Britain had been in the grip of one of its most severe winters in living memory. Snow, Ice and bitter cold didn't deter them. What, then, had they gone for? In the words of Conwy Club secretary Laurence Irving, they had come for a bowl of soup and a simple tin badge.

But that was far from the whole truth. Ask any Dragonist for his impressions. First he will recall the experience of meeting hundreds of friends-friends he may never have met before the camaraderie, the unity.

He will describe the glittering headlight parade by well over 200 machines, the stirring community singing on the castle's Italian marble staircase, the bonfire that out did November fifth. And, not by any means least, he will recall the rousing tones of the rallies most celebrated visitor, Ernst Leverkus from Germany.

Between four o'clock on Friday afternoon and half-past ten on Saturday night, exactly 2,369 keen types passed the control caravan. There they got their lapel badges and tickets for a warming bowl of soup. Soon tents were being pitched and fires kindled. Those without tents dumped their bedrolls in one of the lofty rooms of Gwrych Castle.

The court of the Dragon was in session. Everyone was discussing the ride up. Those who had set out on Saturday morning were surprised to hear that the slushy roads they had encountered had been, only a few hours before, sheets of black ice. The night owls, such as Tiny Tanner of the Oxford Sidecar Club, on the other hand, were chuffed at having clashed with, and beaten, winters worst.

None had conquered the Horseshoe Pass- some adventurous type had set out to try, but were stopped by drifts-and the R.A.C.'s alternative route through Corwen and Cerrigy-druidion was relatively trouble free.

Some had special tales to tell. Ulrich Schwab, for instance, had had an eventful journey on a B.M.W. R69S outfit. He was bowling along the M1 with his two friends when he ran on to reserve and had to turn off at the next exit. No Fuel station was to be seen so Ulrich asked directions of a 16 year-old lad. In no time the boy recognized them as Dragonists. He took them home to meet his father, John Watts- an enthusiast even then preparing for Gwrych. The Germans were invited to stay the night!

At one o'clock on Sunday morning three begrimed enthusiasts arrived to ask if they were too late to check in. They had pushed their broken down outfit for a full 30 miles!

Of one thing all were agreed- the trip to Gwrych had been bitterly cold. Cafe's along the A5 and A55 were invaded by cold and hungry motor cyclists as soon as their doors opened on Saturday morning.

"What's this, then; a rally they're having?" asked one proprietor at St. Asaph, her cafe bulging at the windows.

Rally indeed! from St. Asaph, where the northern and southern routes converged, the Dragon men formed a never ending stream. There was a day-long traffic jam at the castle control.

The talk of motor cycling, motor cyclists and motor cycles went on until the light began to fade. Then camp fires were encouraged and soon a cheerful glow illuminated the Dragons' pitch in the castle grounds. Time for the headlight parade.

Bang on 7.30, Conwy clubman Don Williams led the way, followed by Ernst and Inge Leverkus on their white R69 B.M.W. outfit, Kasawubu. In all, 249 machines solos and outfits filed out of the castle grounds, headlights blazing. They took to the coast road as far as Llandulas and then turned left to Rydd-y-Foel, Making a complete circle of Cefn-yr-Ogof and back to Gwrych.

Snowbound between Ruthin and Wrexham

From the front of the parade the lights stretched for miles, winding in and out of the trees, a vast phosphorescent reptile from a bygone age.

So long was the procession that the leading outfit met the tailenders on the return trip.

When the parade re-entered Gwrych the monster bonfire was well under way. A ring was formed round the fire, and soon the heat became intense. Rumour had it that so well done were the Dragons nearest the blaze that they were served for supper!

RAMPART CALL

Attention was diverted from the fire by a booming voice from the castle ramparts. Ernst Leverkus, father of the Elephant Rally and thus too, through *Motor Cycle,* of the Dragon, was addressing the rallyists. He explained how he wanted to be at the first Dragon but that illness had kept him in Germany. This year he had made it. And he had made 2,500 new friends at the same time!

Ernst Leverkus is presented with a badge by Tiny Tanner on behalf of the Federation of Sidecar Clubs.

Although the headlight parade was something that the riders wouldn't have missed for all the soup in Gwrych, the community singing on the massively proportioned grand staircase was the jollification of the evening. "Illkley Moor", " Luvverly bunch of coconuts", "Enry the Eighth ;" they ran through all the favourites-and a few new ones such as Bill Humes " Song of the Dragon Men"-with the aid of an electronic organ atop the staircase.

The organist had to play 20 encores before he could strike up Auld Lang Syne!

Hardly had the last strains died than tired Dragons were jumping into there bedrolls. Others stayed up all night, talking round the fires. Most had Ernst Leverkus' speech at the back of their minds It sums up, only too well, the real spirit of the Dragon Rally:

"We are like the old sailing men who cannot sit in houses when the wind is singing over the roads and the world is full of fair adventures, and when the sounds of roaring waves call to men....Three cheers to the Conwy Club and the Dragon men, who light the bonfire of motor cycling as it was never before!"

On the fields of Gwrych Castle the Dragonists make their camp for the night.

Courtesy of the 'Motor Cycle'

DRAGNET

By about midnight on the Saturday Conwy Club officials packed up recording details of arrivals. But riders continued to check in and the total number at Gwrych must of topped 2,500.

The last were two Surrey pals, Martin Cairns, 21 , From Sutton, and Peter Trinick, 20, from Banstead, with their 1949 three-fifty Ariel Red Hunter outfit. An Oil flooded magneto had delayed them a long time at Worcester. They fixed it, took a short kip then pressed on to reach Gwrych at 11.10 Sunday Morning! An hour or so later they were heading south proudly displaying their Dragon badges.

A spot of bother along the way. But there were plenty of helping hands, and ice and snow could not stop the enthusiasts keeping their annual rendezvous.

A Dragonist, who shall be nameless, was warming his rump and got too near the pressure stove. More than his pants were burned, the hospital reported. Spurning offers of lifts in sidecars, our hero stuck layers of sponge rubber on the seat of his big Vincent and started for home. He motored out of Gwrych standing on the footrests.

There were plenty of remarkable coincidences such as the meeting of Ulrich Schwab and his pals with the son of a Dragonists father. Here is just one. Three soloists were stopped with a minor bother on the way up from London. A sidecarists pulled up to give a hand.

Next day when returning the soloists stopped to help a sidecarist tinkering on the roadside. You've guessed right . It was the Good Samaritan of the day before.

Some of the campers were enjoying Eskimo life so much they stayed another night and took off for home on the Monday. Short-time factory working has its compensations......

Who made the longest mainland trek to the Dragon? The record awards that honour to a chap named Falconer living in Portsoy on the shore of the Moray Firth, Banffshire. His two way journey was all of 1,000 miles. Other long distance types came from Hawick, Glasgow, and Edinburgh, and there were a few from Cornwall (approaching 350 miles each way). Of course those from the Continent had a 600 mile round gallop from Dover plus the mileage on the other side of Channel. The obvious question now is who made the shortest journey? That's easy. There were two entries from Abergele, within walking distance of the castle!

Conwy boys have already met to discuss next years Dragon. It will be Gwrych again on a weekend in February. Among the plans are a public-address system wired to outside the castle so that those on the terraces can join in the singsong; the bonfire on the slope near the castle instead of on the lower field; more snack bars.

Courtesy of 'The Motor Cycle'

THE ROAD TO THE DRAGON

Llangollen High Street. Heading to the Dragon. Taken by Ray Hughes.

Gosh, that was a trip that was to Gwrych Castle! Fog-black ice slush-snowdrifts-blizzards:every conceivable winter hazard except driving rain. If you weren't an all weather rider when you set off on the Dragon Rally, you sure were by the time you got back!

My Ariel Leader clocked 510 miles and many riders made an even longer journey.

The weekend of the Dragon gave a classic illustration of how winter road conditions can fluctuate even in a country as compact as ours. On the Friday afternoon I left London bathed in bright sunshine. But along the M1 patches of fog were already thickening. As night fell, the menace of black ice struck with hair-raising suddenness.

From Atherstone it took me nearly three hours to reach my night stop at Wellington, some 45 miles away.

Next morning, as soon as we turned the corner into the hills after Chirk-bonk!- snow at last.

The white stuff lay heavily about the surrounding fields and ridges of slush bespattered the road.

At Llangollen the sign said “Horseshoe Pass Closed,” but of course I had to make sure for myself. Even at the foot of the pass it was as though the brief thaw had never been. Above the Britannia Inn, roadside drifts stood 6ft high; underfoot, the virgin snow was 6in deep.

When I met a trials sidecar turning back I decided to call it a day. The Landlady at the Britannia told me that over the top the drifts were 15ft high and that a County Council Caterpillar tractor had to give up in disgust.

Yet as I ate my lunch, several riders passed the Inn, heading with grim determination towards the summit. Did they get through? Are they still there? I didn’t see them come back!

The diversion through Corwen, right along the A494 to Ruthin, was a piece of cake; despite the higher altitude there was less snow than at Llangollen. And from Denbigh to the coast snow and frost seemed almost nil.

Going home, I took the low-lying road through Rhydymwyn (of short-circuit fame), Mold and Wrexham. But the local authorities had been less enthusiastic about road clearing, and ridges of hard frozen slush kept the speed down to 30 m.p.h.

Some heroic types took the A525, the Ruthin-Wrexham road, which skirts the north side of the Horseshoe Pass. Luckily for them the snowplough arrived at the critical moment.

Plans are being hatched. Members of the Conway Club pictured at Gwrych Castle last week

BACK into England once more it seemed our troubles were over, but at the beginning of the M1 the first snowflakes began to fall, and they came thicker and thicker. On such a wide, straight road this sort of going is at least bearable; a steady 35 m.p.h. could be held with confidence.

The driving snow brought yet another hazard. Persistent misfiring pulled me up to clean away the congealed slush around the h.t cable. All along the M1 I had passed halted riders, singly or grouped round a silent model. Were they, too, discovering that an all-weather motor cycle should be as waterproof as a trials plot?

Written by John Ebbrell

Your hosts for the weekend! A happy bunch of Conway clubmen, pictured on the snow-covered battlement of Gwrych

Courtesy of the 'Motor Cycle'

ONE MAN'S DRAGON MEET IS ANOTHERS.......
Letters page from Motor Cycle 21 February 1963

Thanks to all those who gave up their free time for months to make the 1963 Dragon a wonderful success- the Conwy Club. To see such a great gathering of motor cyclists enjoying every minute of the company of fellow riders, not forgetting the boys from Germany, was a sight that will be long remembered by me.
Bill Hume and R.L Miller are to be complimented on composing the " Song of the Dragon Men". I am sure it will be in the Top Ten of Dragon men throughout the world of motor cycling.
A. Shinzil ,Cambridge

ENTHUSIAST

So ,to be defined as a keen enthusiast one has to go to the Dragon Rally (Challenge of The Dragon, February 7). Although I have been motor cycling only four years, with 54,000 miles behind me I consider myself as much as an enthusiast as your so called Dragon Types.

Surely Harry Louis can't be serious when he writes "......... and with any luck we would have to battle through really deep drifts..." (February 7). Statements like this can do nothing but harm to our cause.

The right weather, the open road and a good machine is surely the right way to enjoy to the full this wonderful sport that belongs to every one of us who has a motor cycle.
T. Burgoyne , Belfast

HELPING HANDS

To five Coventry men who were riding a Matchless single, a twin and a Greeves at the Dragon Rally goes our thanks. They not only helped replace a broken chain but, on hearing that we were short of sleeping gear, offered to lend us blankets and a tent.
A.J.S and B.S.A , Leeds.

COMPLEX

I agree with "Enthusiast" (February 7), who condemned the Dragon Rally in weather such as we have been having as foolish. Off-hand, I cannot think of anything which could have been more expressly designed to convince the general public that motor cyclists are completely mad.

Is all this display of "toughness" and "enthusiasm" just a stunt dreamed up by riders to pander to a massive collective inferiority complex brought upon us by the fact that we are criticized right and left by other road users?

Harry Louis said (February 7) he hoped for the worse possible conditions on the roads to Gwrych Castle. Nobody is going to tell me that a solo is the safest machine on ice. I myself am no fair-weather motor cyclist but I cut my riding to a minimum when-ever there is ice or snow about.
L. Tattersall, London, W.C.1.

THE LURE OF THE DRAGON

How wrong can you be? Predictions for the crowd at last weekend's Dragon Rally set 4,000 as a possibility. Too few by more than 1,000. Nobody expected the snow and ice of last year, but did bank on the weather been wet and, probably cold. Wrong again; North Wales was almost warm, with hours of sunshine and hardly a rustle of wind. Arrangements were made for about 2,000 campers with their own tents. Wrong for a third time. The number was nearer 3,000!

Yes this year's Dragon at Gwrych Castle was a record smasher in every way. There may never be another quite like it.

Numbers could well continue to mount, but such balmy weekend weather can surly never occur twice in a century.

Homegoing Dragonists pause for a breather on the summit of The Horseshoe Pass

Mainlanders from as far north as Inverness and as far south as Penzance; Irishmen from the north and south; Austrians, Belgians, Germans, Swedes and Swiss-over 70 altogether from across the water-made the big trek.

All reported wonderful rides to buoy the spirit and make you vow again that there never could be such a grand sport as motor cycling.

Riding home on Sunday was as just as exhilarating.

Without this riding plus, last weekend was as inspiring as ever: the true enthusiast's call from Elephantman Ernst Leverkus, the 500-strong headlamp parade, the mighty bonfire, the sing-song in the castle, the nattering round camp fires. Finally another plus- Father Bill Shergold conducting a " real fellowship" service on Sunday morning. As he put it, to join the Dragon Rally and know what true comradeship means, is to "catch a tiny feeling of Heaven".

That famous Brough addict and vintage authority, Titch Allen said, " Every year the Dragon enriches one's spirit; the chaps here are the salt of the earth."

The "59 Club" members at the Dragon Rally 1964.
With the Rev Bill Shergold on the Right hand side.

THE DAY OF THE DRAGON

You know the quotation: Water, water everywhere nor any drop to drink. Well, it had a rueful meaning for Dieter Kaufmann from Hanover. His sidecar wheel came off second best from an over-enthusiastic encounter with a roadside bank round Cefn-yr-Ogof.

He'd be all right, you say, with a choice from one of the many sidecar-carried BMW spare wheels. Poor Dieter! His bike is a Horex.....

By the way, Dieter has the "distinction" of been the first arrival at Gwrych. He checked in on Wednesday! That's what easy weather does. He had started early in the week as a precaution against the sort of going we had last year.

Two Midlanders pitched their tent as dusk fell on Saturday. One of them went to look for brew-up water. When he hadn't returned after a couple of hours, his friend reported him lost. A call went out but still the missing Dragonist didn't appear.

At ten o'clock on Sunday morning the two pals bumped into each other on the castle terrace. Though he had searched all night the missing camper had been quite unable to locate his tent. He hadn't found the water either!

Providence is not to be tempted, even at the Dragon." How many breakdowns shall we stop for?" asked a humourous rider of his passenger on starting out. Almost needless to say, the first they saw was their own.

Welcome nightcap before turning in.

If you want to hear the lurid stories of snow-bound roads you must meet a 1962 Dragonist. Only report of the white stuff came from Gerhard Monourek, who brought a seven-fifty Harley solo from Vienna. " After Munchen (Munich to us), roads icy and a bit of snow," he said.

You Londoners who made the diversion round by the Oxfordshire sidecar Club's Dragons' Brew-how many more miles longer do you think it was than the M1 run?

John Ebbrell's speedo showed 245 miles from Ilford to Gwrych via the M1 and A5 -and 248 returning by way of Wolverhampton, Birmingham and Oxford.

Ready with a smile, a word, Soup, the bangers and tea, the Oxfordshire lads and lassies welcomed nearly 500. " Last year we only had half that number," quipped chairman Jack Gibbs," but then, the lads needed the grub twice as much."

Harry Louis, though, clocked 233 miles from South London to Gwrych on the M1-A5 route; 252 on the return by way of Shrewsbury, Worcester, Oxford. Fact is, the welcome at Oxford would be worth far, far more miles than that.

A trickle on Friday, a torrent on Saturday; and even on Sunday morning they still kept coming through the main gate. Just about the last to sign in for the coveted Dragon badge were two lads from Walsall at noon. Final count of bodies shattered all previous attendances: 5,044.

ABSENTEE chafing at the bit was Pekka Suuronen, who sent the Conwy Club " motor-cycle spirited greetings from Finland." But next year Pekka hopes to swap his continental one-two-five for a British bigster. Says he, a team of wild horses couldn't then keep me away. And I promise to tempt some other boys with me."

Ken Craven arrived at the Dragon on his well-equipped AJS outfit, it caused quite a bit of interest-especially from two types who surveyed the panniers closely. Said one to the other, " Here's another bloke using Craven gear!"

Coincidences come by the billy-canful. Manfred Berg and his friends from Germany met staffman Mike Evans' Father at the M1 service station on Friday night. A few words in German and Manfred was dispatched with a message to the son at the Dragon. But it transpired that Manfred was the first Dragonist Mike Evans chatted with when he reached North Wales. The Germans were able to hand over the greeting " viele grusse von dad" (many greetings from your dad)..

Youngest ever Dragonist, seven month-old Nigel Kay from Maidstone.

Smart get-up worn by Helmut Modro and Bernd Missfield were green uniforms of the West German police. At work they patrol on BMW outfits, but they travelled to North Wales on their private BM sidecar.

When they arrived at Gwrych they were well entertained by Abergele police-and slept in the local station until they left for Germany at 2am on Sunday morning. Why the rush? Duty called at Cologne carnival on Monday morning.

With attendance about 1,000 more than expected, the Conwy Club can be excused for running out of badges (and free soup, too!). The later arrivals, who were the unlucky ones, will receive their badge by post.

Four apprentices from the Norton factory needed transport. The factory chipped in to lend two of the export only seven-fifty Atlases. One was a single carb police model, the other the twin-carb version. But the lads had to keep a tight reign on itching throttle hands. The bikes were brand-new. "Running-in speeds only," said the boss.

So once again another excellent Dragon Rally was enjoyed by enthusiasts from all over the British Isles and the continent. What will next year bring? we shall all have to wait and see.

Courtesy of the 'Motor Cycle'.

DRAGON ACCESSORIES

Compiled by John Ebbrell from the Motor Cycle 1964

Going on the Dragon Rally? You'll have a whale of a time, that we guarantee. But will the ride to Gwrych and the sleeping out prove to be unpleasant? To take the edge off the austerity, I have carefully selected these extras for your machine, your clothing and your overnight stay.

LEAD KINDLY LIGHT.

Left: in this case, a butane lantern, one of the most illuminating inventions any wintertime camper could wish for. This Lumogaz C produces much the same light as a 75-watt bulb-and a fair amount of heat besides. A 3s 6d Camping Gaz cartridge keeps it going for five hours. Imported by the Pneumatic Tent Co, the lantern complete costs: £3 16s

THREE BEAMS IN ONE.

How? Secret of the Raydyot DL 100 is a triple-filament light unit. No 1 beam is a 50-watt long-range driving light; No 2 gives a 40-watt dipped beam; No 3 has a 45-watt flat-top amber beam for use in fog. Lens diameter is 5in. Inclusive of two flick switches and an auxiliary mounting bracket, the DL100 costs £5 12s 6d.

Made by Raydyot, Ltd.

SKATING RAILS.

Minor spills on icy roads? Well designed safety bars can reduce superficial damage to nil proportions. The Britax Senior Front, made from 1in dia 12-gauge tubing, a full hoop pattern, with three-point tailor made attachment brackets, costs £4 8s. Similar price buys Britax Rearguards to protect the stern. These are left-and right-handed bars, which incoporate pillion footrests.

MOBILE KITCHEN.

Around freezing point butane gas is apt to prove Sluggish.. So haute cuisine in low temperatures demands propane gas. Rechargeable cylinders only are the rule: and among the most bijou in the business is the 10oz primus 2000 at a first cost of £2 11s. Here, one is piped up to Falk's compact two-burner Pandora stove. Together with a Primus adaptor, it bears a £6 14s 9d price tag.

WARM HANDS.

Ken Craven offers these electrically heated gauntlets in six-volt or 12 volt versions, wiring harness and postage included for £6 5s. Styled after R.A.F flying gloves, the gauntlets are not at all clumsy in service, but overmitts are helpful for the best results.

From Craven Equipment, Ltd, 61 Eden Grove London, N7

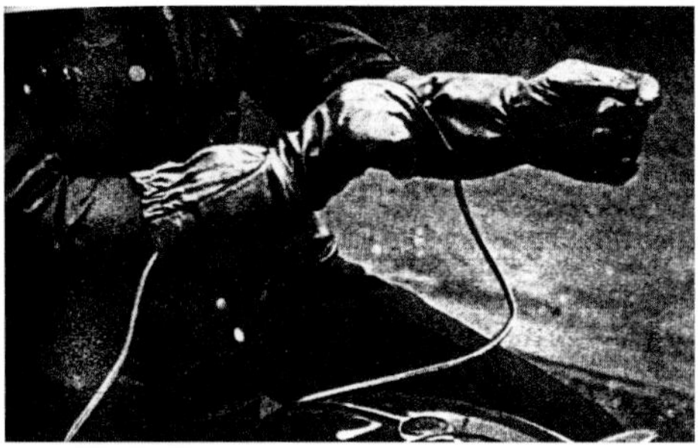

LAP OF LUXURY.

A butane gas-fuelled space heater, believe it or not!
This Prima-camping product is claimed to burn for seven hours on a single 9S 6d cartridge. The assembly weighs only 2lb and dismantles to suitably modest proportions; the cartridge is self-sealing. Price? £4 18s 10d, ready to light.

Imported by Eurafric, Royal Liver Buildings, Liverpool, 3.

UNDERNEATH.

An American import, the Alaska two-piece suit, left, makes cosy wear under the waterproofs. made from lightweight nylon, jacket and trousers are quilted with Dacron synthetic-fibre insulation. both garments are washable. Sizes available: small, medium, large, extra-large, in a choice of six colours. Supplied separately, the jacket costs £3 14s 6d, trousers £2 9s 6d; together £5 19s 6d.

Available only form Badges and Equipment, Ltd, 435, Strand, London, WC2. Postage is 2s 9d on each parcel.

MUMMIFIED.

Quite true, one can make do with blankets and safety pins- but a pukka sleeping bag is so much more comfy. And the more you pay for a sleeping bag the warmer you sleep. An Ice Cap in quilted water-repellent cotton,and duck down filled, costs £7 4s

WHITE OR RED.

Nothing's more annoying than blundering about in a pitch-dark tent. This clever Pifco Motolite above is crocodile-clipped to the battery with 25ft leads.
A switch on the lamp body operates a white floodlight and/or a red flasher dome.
In six volt or 12 volt versions, the Motolite costs 15s 6d.

THE FOURTH DRAGON

Next Saturday is the great day. As dawn breaks over the mountains of Snowdonia, a steady stream of riders will be already climbing the famed Llanberis Pass.

Farther back- beyond Capel Curig, beyond Llangollen, down the A5 into the heart of England-thousands more bring their bikes to life and head westward towards the snow-flecked Welsh hills, until the stream becomes a torrent and the torrent a flood.

This is the day of the Dragon. The Dragon Rally, when all the great-hearted enthusiasts who are proud to call themselves motor cyclists forgather in their thousands for one magnificent weekend.

There are riders from the most distant corners of England and Scotland over the water from the Isle of Man and Ireland, breaking the barriers of language from France, Belgium, Holland, Switzerland, Sweden and above all, Germany where the great *Elefantentreffen* has lighted an answering beacon in the depths of the North Wales hills.

This year, the red-dragon banner floats over Glyn Padarn, Llanberis, at the foot of Snowdon. Shadows lengthen across the still waters of Glyn Padarn, the blaze of the winter sunset dies away behind sharp-edged mountains and a welcoming beacon fire breaks out high above our tents.

Focus for a thousand camp fires, target for the procession of converging headlamps!

There are few entertainments and no luxuries here. Smiling faces, a warm handshake, a cheery welcome have brought this host to such a wild remote spot. Yet the reward is beyond price.

The Dragon Rally Gives two unforgettable days that no true-hearted enthusiast would willingly miss. The camp fires die to embers, the riders melt away to the far corners of Europe. But the flame of friendship, kindled in the North Wales mountains, burns steadily and undimmed-spirit of motor-cycling, the greatest game in the world.

Courtesy of the 'Motor Cycle'

On top of the hill where the beacon will be, John Ebbrell looks down to the trees enclosing the site. In the distance, to the south, is the Llanberis Pass.

BIGGER-THAN-EVER DRAGON RALLY

This fantastic Dragon creation in papier-mache is atop a saloon sidecar.

As ever, the 1965 Dragon Rally was an unparalleled success. over 6,000 enthusiasts poured across the North Wales mountains from all over Britain and the far corners of Europe to join together in this great mid-winter adventure.
The same Dragon, the same cheery faces of the Conwy club to welcome us at journeys end. Yet this year, it was different. This year we had a new site at Glyn Padarn, where thousands of tents perched high on a steep hillside. Instead of a mock-gothic castle as a backcloth,we had the incomparable Snowdon, highest peak in Wales. And what magnificent riding! Longer, colder than last year, but climbing through some of the wildest, most awe-inspiring scenery in Britain.

As usual, this Dragon Rally brought countless stories, some comic, some scarcely less than heroic. Heres one-only one, yet oh so typical of the Dragonists' enthusiasm.

Saturday morning, Tony Norman set off on his Vincent from Fulham. Within 20 miles his gear box suddenly shed all its cogs. So he abandoned everything at a friendly garage-bike, camping gear, food- and set out to hitchhike north. More than 12 hours after leaving home, at last he reached Glyn Padarn.

Without a sleeping bag, without blankets, he spent the night in the open curled up in front of the bonfire.

Next morning he must leave at dawn to make the journey home to London. We discovered him halfway back along the A5. "Why didn't you give up?" we asked him. "Why didn't you go home when you were still so near?" "What!" he cried. "Miss getting my badge? Miss the Dragon? Not on your life, mate!"

Lucky lads those who set out in Friday's daylight. They had a mild dry run to Glyn Padarn. But while the early birds lay snug in their tents that night, their friends were fighting their way through belts of torrential , icy rain.

Buzzard's-eye view of Glyn Padarn camping.

By Saturday morning all was clear. The wind had shifted; one could smell the ozone blowing in from the sea, light snow melted quickly from around the tents. The sun came out and brought a sparkle to the whitened flanks of the mountains that reared up all around us.
Dragon weather indeed!

DESPITE its enormous area, much of the Glyn Padarn site is too steep for pitching tents. A record number of campers arrived, but to the relief of the Conwy Club they all fitted comfortably into place and without guyline tripping over, so prevalent last year at Gwrych. Many Dragonists spoke enthusiastically of the snug mateyness of Glyn Padarn's terraces, with clumps of birch trees to give shelter. Others missed the togetherness of the Gwrych frontage.

Of those without tents, pretty well everybody got shelter of a sort-though by late Saturday they were already hunting for corners in abandoned air-raid shelters and tumbledown barns.

It's always a wild ride to Wales from the North-East. Geordie and North Yorkshire types always have lurid stories of fighting their way over the midwinter Pennines.

Dragon songsmith Bill Hume met rain so cold, on the Friday night, that his 1963 Matchless big twin began to suffer from ice in the carburettor.

When he was on the M6 the moon came out, but beyond Corwen he met " snow and hail like a sandblaster."

At first light, vintage enthusiast Hume discovered a filling-station open, stopped for petrol and spotted a 1929 Coventry-Eagle Flying 8 abandoned and cobwebby in the back.

" I'm going back to see about buying it before I go home," he told us. "Then all I'll need is someone to tiller the device at the far end of my tow-rope."

Right in the middle of Harry Louis' speech of welcome the generator went on the blink-no public-address system, no music from the brass band, no lights. But everyone took the mishap in good part and the power came on about an hour later.

This little episode gives some idea of how much the Conwy Club put into the Dragon.

little jobs like wiring a site, generating juice, laying mains water supplies......

Much-missed; Ernst Leverkus' speech of welcome. The father of the Elephant Rally has been on the sick list for many months now and he is still not yet fit enough to travel.

A wonderful ride to Glyn Padarn? The riders are fighting their way through the teeth of a gale along the lonely road from Capel Curig to the Llanberis Pass.

But, said his wife Inge who deputized for him at the microphone, he should certainly be over in the Island for the Six Days and is furiously arguing with his doctor about going to the TT. Inge, by the way, came to Glyn Padarn under her own steam, driving a BMW outfit the whole way. In the sidecar she brought her mother, who soon became *Omar* (Granny) to her fellow Dragonists.

For nearly half an hour a party of "stokers" worked like slaves to get the ceremonial bonfire going. It was reluctant to take- but when it did it was the biggest, most fiery ever.

So good, in fact, that windborne sparks set two tents alight!

OLD tyres proved superb fuel. One was hooked on the top of the long tree trunk that jutted like a spire from the pile, 45ft above the ground. As this tyre burned it broke away into three rings of fire-the tread and the two walls, but they somehow remained hooked together like the rings of the Olympic symbol.

The loud laugh of Colin "Lefty" Bembridge was much in evidence. Although his right arm is still out of commission, he had driven up from London with his Ariel Four Sidecar oufit.

Midnight, just outside Llangollen, his throttle cable broke. With characteristic determination, Colin tied(one-handed) the inner cable to the chinstrap of his helmet and carried on that way, raising his head for more steam and vice versa to shut off.

The tent is pitched, the kettle boiling, the grub cooked. Now all we need to do is eat!

Plenty of supporters turned up- but someone different was in charge. We're talking about the Sunday-morning service which, in the absence of Father Bill Shergold, was taken by his curate, Graham Hullett.

As might be expected, Father Hullett is as keen as a motor cyclist as they come. He rides a BSA Road Rocket.

First to call on Sunday at the Oxfordshire Sidecar Club's brew-up, in its usual spot on The northern approach to the city, were Inge Leverkus and her mother with their BMW outfit. Althrough the afternoon and evening groups of homeward Dragonists enjoyed the soup and hot-dogs, and warmed their frozen hands in front of sizzling braziers.

This Oxford stop has become a Dragon highlight. Many enthusiasts deviate quite a few miles from their shortest route to call in. Its the last chance for real Dragon atmosphere and for the final " See you next year."

Thanks Lads and lasses of The Oxfordshire Sidecar Club.

Courtesy of the 'Motor Cycle'

Shoulder to Shoulder, perched even in the trees, Dragonists flock to the sing-song round the bonfire. A local silver band provide music for the occasion.

DRAGON TAILS FROM GLYN PADARN 1965

BMW rider Keith Bailey wants to renew acquaintance with fellow enthusiast for the Munich marque. This other chap comes from Nottingham and rides a very fast 1955 R50. Will he please write to Keith at "B" Mess, AERE, Harwell, Didcot, Berks.

Old friends have been inquiring after sidecarrists Tony Luker and Jim McIntyre, who pranged their Royal Enfield outfit on the homeward run near Llangollen.

Tony had only slight injuries and was not detained; Jim suffered a chipped bone in the instep and should have left Oswestry Hospital within the last few days.

Is he the smallest-engined, shortest-stopping Dragonist? G.I. Joyce of Ashton-Under-Lyne Lancs, rode nearly 150 miles to Glyn Padarn on wait for it- a Raleigh moped!

He left home a 8.45pm on the Saturday, and, travelling through the night, arrived at 5.15am the following morning. Two hours later, off he set back to Lancashire, getting home at 3.30pm- in time for work!

We are still hearing from Dragonists writing in appreciation of the fun they had at Glyn Padarn or on the runs there and back. General vote seems to be that it was the best-ever gathering of the clans, with the campers to the fore in their praises.

Of the 6,000 odd who checked in, more than half were under canvas, and the record shows that there were over 2,000 tents. This was a talking point at Glyn Padarn. So was the excellence of much of the camping equipment.

A big thank you goes out to the hard-working members of the Conwy Club. Yes and they are still at work. It will take them a few weekends more before the site is in shipshape order. And thank you is the theme of many of your letters from enthusiasts who struck bother and were helped on the road.

Tony Norman, mentioned in our rally report, was but one of many who blew-up on the outward trip yet got lifts for the remainder of the journey there and home again.

There was at least one-Bill Whittaker of Chorley-who while giving a lift home to another lad in bother, had his own bike conk out.

As the Velo had to be abandoned, Bill found himself on the thumb line. With the help of riders from Leeds and Scunthorpe he made it and really enjoyed the pillion riding.

About the toughest weekend came the way of Bob O'Brien of Sidcup. He set out on Friday night on his 1956 Ariel Red Hunter. All went well to Kidderminster "apart from an 80 mile detour in the Evesham area." As compression had evaporated, Bob stripped off the head and pot. He was soon shopping around for a new piston. He couldn't find one of the right type, but something that was more-or-less suitable was machined to fit in a nearby workshop. Eventually the engine was in one piece but it died again at Gobowen. That was not all. As Bob pushed it in the hope of finding a workshop open- it was by now late on Saturday night-the rear tyre punctured!

he gave up and returned home by train, but between times, he had been helped by "about 103" Dragonists, among them two from the 59 Club. Who were with him for five hours in Kidderminster on the Saturday.

Courtsey of the 'Motor Cycle'

MAKING SURE!

They sure breed enthusiastic riders down Southend way. Last weekend, Ian Buckley and three friends rolled up at the Conwy Club secretary's front door in Llandudno. "We just wanted to make sure of our Dragon entries," they said.

Well it isn't quite necessary to make a 500-mile round trip if you want to guarantee yourself sleeping space under cover at Glyn Padarn, where the 1966 rally was been held.

Though at the weekend, some 2,500 enthusiasts had booked places, the Conwy Club can still make arrangements-provided your entry form is in their hands by next Monday.

They must have notice to hire and erect marquees for the overflow sleepers. That's why after-Monday latecomers must expect pot luck with their kipping-down arrangements, or bring tents.

Latest Dragon news concerns the BMF and Fellowship of Riders, who will be organising their own H.Q.

And Dragonists heading along the A5 haul on Friday may find it a worthwhile diversion to Heath Mill Lane, Birmingham, where Rev David Collyer and the Double Zero Club are preparing a welc-ome at St. Basil's Church Hall.

There'll be sleeping space for up to 400 people, hot drinks and a mechanic all laid on by the local Civil Defence people- even an interpreter for French and German. St. Basil's just off the A45 Coventry road, is easy to find.

St Basil's will open also on Sunday from midday till 10.30pm. Anyone is welcome.

APPLICATION FORM FOR ASSOCIATE MEMBERSHIP OF THE CONWAY AND DISTRICT MOTOR CYCLE CLUB

DRAGON RALLY

4–6 FEBRUARY 1966

☐ I will be camping ☐ Accommodation wanted

MARK the appropriate square above with a tick, Then cut out this form and post it, together with your subscription of 10s, to this address:

L. M. Irving, Beech Grove, 32, St Mary's Road, Llandudno, North Wales.

Postal orders should be made payable to the Conway and DMCC. Please enclose a stamped, addressed envelope for your receipt and admission ticket.

Will you bring a passenger? If so, a separate application form must be completed.

Do you want to be booked in with a party? NO/YES with details:

....

I agree that the Conway and DMCC, Glen (Caernarvon), Ltd, "Motor Cycle" and their respective officials will be under no liability for any injury or damage to me or my property or my passengers, howsoever caused, at this rally.

SIGNATURE..

NAME (capitals please)..

ADDRESS ....

....

....

MACHINE (make and registration number)...........................

And our good friends the Oxfordshire Sidecar Club are once again doing their Sunday bangers and rolls on the A34 just North of Oxford.

Dragons Brew sets up shop from 1pm and closes when the grub runs out. So see you at the Dragon and a safe journey too you all.

GLYN PADARN OR BUST!

That's the favourite slogan of any enthusiast heading an ancient motor bike to the Dragon Rally. And it staggers the imagination just how many really do go bust. Every year we could fill *Motor Cycle* from cover to cover with stirring tales of the heroic efforts made to revive sick machinery to get to North Wales and back home again.

So this year I set off with photographer David Allen ensconced in the sidecar of a Triumph Watsonian GP. Our job? To get the fullest possible story of individual Dragon Breakdowns. The joke (a sick joke too!) was that those tatty old rips hardly came into the picture. Almost without exception, the broken down machines were relatively new models.

There is always a helping hand when you breakdown on the way to the Dragon Rally.

So why did so many fall by the wayside? From what we saw, the answer is harsh and unmistakeable-because they neglect essential maintenance. Probing behind the reasons why I heard stories of last minute major rebuilds, of secondhand models unchecked since their previous owner. I met riders who had only the vaguest idea of even the first step to take when tracing troubles by the roadside.

Now lets begin with the likeliest,the most obvious of all roadside calamities, a puncture. This is a classic example where the job is perfectly straightforward if you've got the right tools and utterly hopeless if you haven't.

The wheel has to come out so you need spanners (hefty spanners, capable of the effort, please note) and maybe pliers for the chain spring link; the cover must come off, so you want tyre levers, at least two, and a valve-core key.

Through one of the occasional spots of sunshine, Dragonists wend their way homeward. This is at Capel Curig where they turn right on to the A5.

And when it comes to the actual repair, it's not much good if you've lost the patches and the solution tube has deteriorated to a shrivelled husk. Finally, even a new tube will stay obstinately flat if you have no pump.

Almost the first casualty I encountered was a rear-wheel puncture. Dave Evans and his girlfriend Marilyn Taylor, marooned with an A7 BSA twin on the M1.

DUCKS AND DRAGONS

The Conwy Club's Dragon seems to have the bit between its teeth. Every year it forges farther ahead. The attendance goes up and up. Last weekends get-together at the foot of Snowdon numbered at least 6,420 and the final reckoning may be higher.

Yet the weather was the most uninviting so far. The previous four rallies have been held in heavy snow, ice tingling cold and brilliant sunshine. For this, the fifth, no one escaped the rain, floods, mist and galeforce winds, though temperatures were quite high for February.

Yet even this sort of depressing weather had it's compensations. Rivers and streams became raging torrents as boisterous and foaming and spectacular as those in the French or Swiss Alps when the snow melts in spring.

Every so often along the roads leading to Glyn Padarn, groups of Dragonists stopped at the roadside to gaze in awe at the raging waters-this part of the tourists' attractions of North Wales were never so splendid in the holiday season.

How you fared through the Llanberis Pass depended on the day and the time. The early birds who made Glyn Padarn on Friday swooped through lengths of flooded road and gusty side winds so strong that it was impossible to avoid wavering from side to side.

During the night the wind dropped and a wet and clammy mist closed in. At times it was so thick that a bottom-gear crawl was the only way to sort out the turns. And on Saturday when the big intake went through you could meet mist, lashing rain or a burst of wintery sunshine!

No matter: spirits were as buoyant as always at Glyn Padarn with tents filling every suitable plot of ground. Only the small camp fires suffered, for it was a problem to get sodden wood to make a friendly flare.

Would the dampness spoil the traditional bonfire that marks the high spot of the Dragon Saturday-night festivities? Not Likely! With a spot of petrol to give it a whoosh the pyre was soon going, sending flames high in the air.

The rain was now holding off. First the headlight parade with such a long cavalcade of lamps stabbing the darkness that the circuit looked like a ring of fire.

Next came the welcomes. First from "Tiger" Roberts, chairman of the Conwy Club. Then from Harry Louis who brought a personal message from the new Minister of Transport, Mrs. Barbara Castle.

Led by the Llandulas Choir the Saturday sing-song gets under way. No mistaking the choir members-they're in Civvies!

A SPECIAL greeting to the Germans- the biggest contingent, with over 60, from the Continent-read in their language by Mike Evans and, finally, a brief blessing from Father Graham Hullett of the 59 Club.

By eight o'clock the famous Llandulas Choir was leading the singing. When they had had enough there were plenty of others to take over with impromptu community songs. For nearly three hours the valley echoed with lusty voices. Much, much later the last of the lights went out. The night was so mild that you could walk around in shirtsleeves as your riding gear dried out. Mild -and dry-next morning, too.

Sharing a Tiger cub are Pat Wilde, who brought her husband to the rally on the pillion seat, and on the back seat Barbara Knowles. Both active in the Lancs section of the VES.

Though nobody had a completely dry run home whether he went north east or south. But the showers were rarely heavy and when the sun broke through it reminded you that spring is not far away...

On the Thursday evening before the rally, the Oxfordshire Sidecar Club hosted nine German rallyists at their HQ. Jack Gibbs then arranged a tour of the Triumph factory for the following day. It proved so popular that it was a job to drag the Germans away and get them to Glyn Padarn.

Earlier they had been very impressed by the English police after asking a patrolman in London to tell them the route to Oxford.

He jumped on his Triumph and gave them the red-carpet escort treatment all the way to the M4!

What was the most unusual registration number? All the old faithfuls were there, including the Harley-Davidson with the Canadian registration. But the rather oriental-looking number with CFS nationality plate set us thinking. The owner of the beige coloured BMW R69S and Steib was 38 year old Lieutenant Francois Barret, a friend of Jean-Marie Debonneville, and the machine hailed from French Somaliland on the shores of the Red Sea! However, Lieut Barret had been staying a month or two at his home in Bordeaux, so the feat wasn't so astounding as it at first appeared. Nevertheless, it was a fair ride to Wales. Getting to the Dragon and dealing with the sort of road side bothers that can occur is essentially a man's game. But there were a number of ladies who made Glyn Padarn on their own mounts-like 25 year old Ruth Knight of Chelmsford on her 1961 Triumph T110 and Canterbury chair.

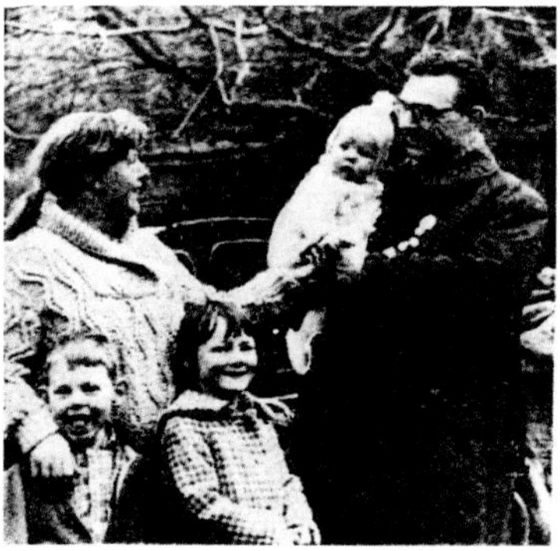

Youngest ever resident at Glyn Padarn, 4 1/2 month old Robert Johnson with Mum, Dad, Peter and Paula.

After setting off at 11pm on Friday, she arrived at the rally just 24 hours later. She stopped to help several unfortunates by the side of the road during the early hours of Saturday morning and then found herself in serious trouble at Wellington. The back wheel of the Triumph had collapsed. Ruth and passenger Bernard Cramer spent the best part of the day rebuilding the wheel.

EXCERPTS from Mrs Barbara Castle's special message of welcome to the rally;
" I share your love of outdoor life and admire your enthusiasm for your sport. Enthusiasm and skill go together. The man for whom motor cycling is part of the open air life is likely to be skilled in roadcraft."
" I hope you will demonstrate your skill in the best possible way-by setting an example to others. I hope you will do this in the same spirit of comradeship shown at this rally, by teaching others to take care of their machines and to take care on the roads.
Good luck to you all"

We hear a great deal about visitors from the continent-yet a sadly neglected contingent from over the water is the Irish one.
However, all our friends from Ireland, like 20 year old Lionel Watts of Limerick, were pleased to hear Harry Louis mention them in his speech.

Wellington boots were selling well in Llanberis. The stock of popular sizes had all but gone by early Saturday afternoon. Fresh supplies were soon coming in from Caernarvon.

"Well worth opening-up. We were all very happy with what was achieved." So reported David Collyer, of the Birmingham Double Zero Club's enterprise in putting club head-quarters, St. Basil's Church Hall, at the disposal of Dragon rallyists. In all, 162 riders dropped in for coffee or soup on the way to Glyn Padarn-among them nine German's and four Swedish visitors, and Norwegian and French pairs. Not everybody stopped the night, but those who did used their bed rolls in the centrally heated hall, numbered 53. Says David Collyer: " Some got their heads down just for a few hours, and I was making wakey-wakey calls. By prior arrangement, right through the night. The last caller arrived at 8.15 on Saturday morning, just in time for breakfast!"

As they tucked into their four-course Saturday dinner, Motor Cycles team under canvas thought themselves in the Dragon camper's Ritz. But even the luxuries of table, stools and propane lantern paled into insignificance against Norman Chadderton's caravan. It was a genuine four- berth model, a lightweight Travelette. Norman's 1957 Square Four did the donkey work of getting the caravan over from Shaw, Lancs. Three lucky friends had come along to share the cosy pleasures of this moblie home.

The Oxfordshire Sidecar Club a Dragon's Brew, with soup, hotdogs and thawing out brazier, makes a welcome break for homegoing rallyists.

The detail that we liked best was the neatly laid out row of four pairs of carpet slippers!
Contingents from abroad were the biggest so far. They came from Austria, Belgium, Holland, France,Germany (including Berlin), Luxembourg, Norway and Switzer-land. Among the many club contigents were Vintage and Brough Superior. Rim brakes and rain never went well together but that didn't stop the riders of the older vintage bikes making it. Broughs? well, they attracted as much attention as the 1966 jobs, including at least four CB450 Honda's. First arrivals came on the Wed-nesday. The last checked in at 11.30 am on Sunday after a series of breakdowns that delayed him all Sat-urday night.

ON SUNDAY morning, Birge Paulsen, riding a 1938 seven-fifty BMW, popped up at the control caravan. "Hello", he said, " I'd like to have the farthest-travelled rallyist award please. I've come all the way from Norway specially because I knew this was one prize I would win." Gently, Conwy Club officials took Birge to one side, to explain there just weren't any awards at all; only little enamel badges.......

Although somewhat off the beaten track for most Dragonists, the Oxfordshire Sidecar Club's brew-up and thaw-out station near the Oxford by-pass drew its usual crowd of thankful patrons. All Sunday afternoon and evening it was thronged with homegoing rallyists who'd called in for a last natter and a joke together. No precise count was taken but, says secretary Roger Green, "We got rid of 500 rolls and 28lb of sausages." A few callers puzzled over the reason why the brazier and hot-dog stand had been set up on the "wrong" side of the road. The reason is simple: the wrong side has the right kind of farmer who allows the Oxfordshire Club to set up shop on a short stretch of private track. More than that, this gentleman puts forward his good offices to the extent of lending the club a redundant milk churn as a water tank and storing the gear in his barn. One after dark visitor, determined to prove the opposite side of the road would serve just as well, set out to do some surveying on his own account. Imagine the consternation of the Oxfordshire sidecarrists when their "helper" suddenly vanished into an 8ft-deep drainage channel! his bike was a little damaged, but the rider went off to hospital with a suspected shoulder dislocation. Most waggish remark of the afternoon? "It's so warm today, you ought to be serving ices, not hot bangers!

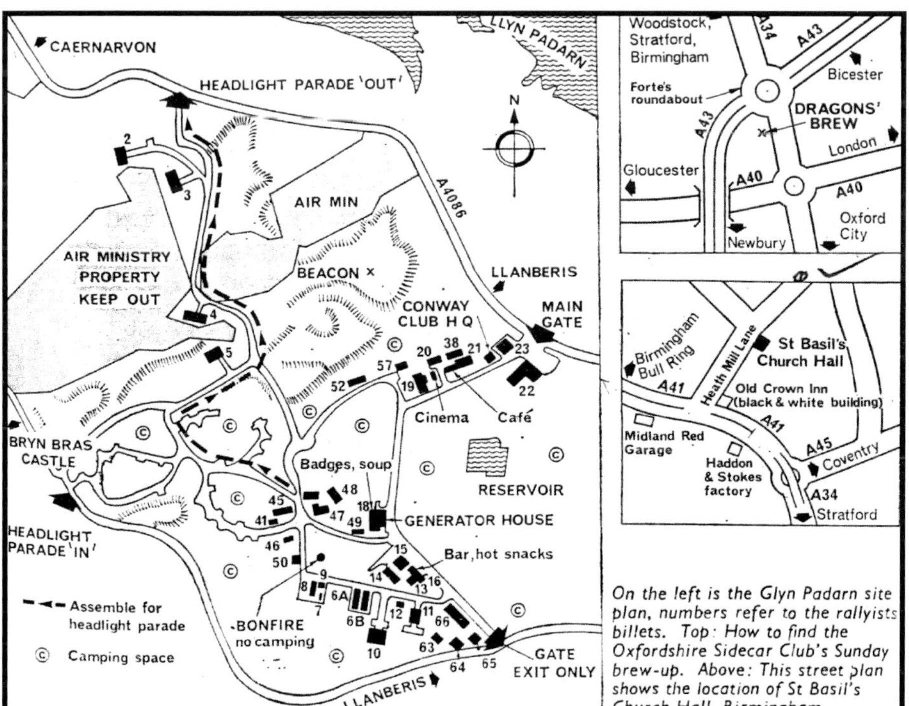

On the left is the Glyn Padarn site plan, numbers refer to the rallyists billets. Top: How to find the Oxfordshire Sidecar Club's Sunday brew-up. Above: This street plan shows the location of St Basil's Church Hall, Birmingham

Courtesy of the 'Motor Cycle'

CHASING THE DRAGON 1966

Snaking their way through the Pass is some Dragon Rally riders.

Everyone had a whale of a time at this year's Dragon Rally; but lets face it, there were a few weeds lurking 'mid the garden flowers. The gay young gent with what sounded like an Ariel Arrow on open pipes decided, for the Third year in succession, to do a bit of throttle tuning at midnight. Worse, the local papers fell with glee on the parties of roisterers in Llanberis.

There were reports of scuffles with the police, souvenir hunters on the scrounge, glasses smashed in public houses, noise. Well ,maybe some of this was a bit exaggerated; but even if the roughnecks numbered a mere 30 or 40 out of 6,400 honest Dragonists, its still 30 or 40 too many. So how do we get rid? The Conwy Club are as eager as anybody to clear out the anti-social element. They thought they had done that by forbidding entry to cars and vans, and moving the Dragon site to the other side of the mountains. So their secretary, Lawrence Irving, wants suggestions. If you've got any constructive ideas, send them to his address. But try to keep within the spirit of the Dragon Rally.

Many people would of voted the 1966 Dragon Rally the best ever-a record crowd and the organisation well jacked up. Alas, there was a tragedy for the 59 Clubmen Roger Fellows and Arthur Batho. The facts are these. After checking in at Glyn Padarn they set out on Saturday morning for the ride back through the Llanberis Pass. A storm had blown up that morning and over the far side of the pass it was like a hurricane. On the exposed stretch of road between Pen -y- Gwryd and Capel Curig, a sudden gust of wind blew them off course, straight into the path of an oncoming German BMW sidecar outfit.

As might be expected, the Sunday press (which up till now have virtually ignored the Dragon), not to speak of one of *Motor Cycle's* competitors, fastened on the tragedy. But in all justice one should see it in perspective. These are the first fatalities I have heard of in the five Dragon Rallies. This year's event attracted over 6,000 enthusiasts-say 4,000 machines altogether. Assuming that the average rider did a round trip of 250 miles (a very conservative estimate I should say) that would make a total of 1,000,000 riders miles. So in cold figures, the average was one fatality in half a million miles, or about two million miles for the entire series of rallies. That is a fantastically good record and astonishingly better than the national average I have seen published for any type of vehicle.

Written By John Ebbrell

TO WALES WITH AN ELDERLY DRAGON

The idea of trekking 150 miles to camp overnight on a bleak hillside in the middle of winter has, for five years, struck me as a particularly crackpot one. Snowdonia may be attractive but to my mind camping is something for boy scouts. Bitter memories of my one and only camping holiday come flooding back....... try to knock tent pegs into a wet sandy soil at 4am, in the teeth of a north westerly gale, when clad only in pyjamas and an all too inadequate raincoat; finding "things" in the sugar; finding water in the bed....for camping, count me out! And please don't write offering me advice, free loan of equipment, or what have you. For my holiday I like a warm bed, a "cuppa" in the morning, radio and phone in the bedroom and a waterproof roof. You enjoy camping-good show, there wouldn't be enough hotels to go round if nobody camped.

Even so a steady recital over the years from colleagues C.E.A and F.P.M. of the camaraderie-cum-bonhomie of the Dragon Rally made me realise that, possibly, I was missing something. For five years I had expounded the theory that it was possible to do the rally on a veteran combination but my colleagues were getting a little bit tired of this hot air and fairly obviously expected no action. Stung by their lack of attention when I said, for the fifth time, that my 1914 sunbeam outfit would laugh at Snowdon, I decided that perhaps I was not indispensable to my antique business, that I could take a day and a half off.

Stephen(10) who went to the Dragon, and June (2)and Carol (4) who didn't... and the Sunbeam.

I was confident that we should have good weather if I rode, for it was well known that the sun always shines on the righteous. ..February came and, come Tuesday before Rally Saturday, I dashed to Stamford Hall to resume the outfit (the museum does not open until Easter Sunday so it wouldn't be missed) and sent off my entry form together with fees for myself and 10 1/2-year-old S. J. G. Having called my own bluff, I set to and agglomerated what equipment I could. In the event we took one outfit, two people, three blankets, one car rug, two sleeping bags, two spirit stoves (we used neither), a gallon can of petrol, enough food to enable us to have sustenance if we had to walk all 300 miles, and enough tools to strip thc bike if necessary.

Careful, studied conversation with a more virile neighbour confirmed that it got light at about 7.am, and so, to my secret disgust, Stephen and I were eating bacon and eggs at 6.30 a.m on a Rally Saturday. Outside, the grey dawn turned into a wet grey fog and promptly, half-an-hour late (it's prompt for me), I wrapped Stephen in an ex-police raincoat, jammed him into the sidecar, and we were ready to go.

The Sunbeam started easily- I have regularly won "tanner" bets for first-kick starting in the cold, which is more than most Velo owners can say (apparently).

I HAD hardly ridden a bike in 1966 (800 miles on a certain 450 and perhaps 200 on various others counts as "hardly" for me, but the rhythmic beat of the 770 c.c J.A.P. vee-twin seemed to sweep away the cobwebs in a minute.

It was still only half light and we got several long stares from half-awake people as we motored through the villages to reach the A5, main artery of the Dragons life blood. Past the woodyard in Claybrooke Magna- the editor's Essex, has some interesting names but none to compare with those of Leicestershire, favoured county of three contributors at least-and up the long hill to High Cross.

This is the old "centre of England" where the Romans' Watling Street was crossed by the Fosse Way. History does not record the outcome but a (High) Cross marks the spot.

Very little time for thoughts of the Romans as we groped through the cold and clammy fog.

With enthusiasm of youth, Stephen proclaimed that he wasn't cold-his dad was already bitterly regretting his rash boasting of how easy this "kids" run would be on a Veteran. I'm not sure if it's better to get colder quicker for a short time on a new bike, or to freeze gradually for a long time on a near-antique.

Soon after passing the Hinkley Knight roundabout, the Sunbeam showed unmistakable signs of a blocked jet. Just before the start of the Atherstone by-pass I pulled into a layby to clean the carburetter-a job that should of been done before we started. Twenty minutes wasted before we were away again. I really must get a spanner that fits those square-head nuts on the B. and B. carburettor a "work bench wisdom" prize pair of multi-grip pliers is not really the correct tool for the job.

Twenty miles on came a suggestion of another blocked jet so I tried full throttle in the hope that the offending particles would pass. They did not and the outfit surged forward.

Unfortunately, the throttle was stuck wide but mercifully the valve lifter worked. Appropriately we were near Hints, a village that must suggest a lot of puns but I can't think of one at the moment.

Past the Gailey roundabout, and I recalled that it had been said in '*Motor Cycle*' that someone would be dishing out tea in 10 miles. Sure enough they were and to my surprise and pleasure it was *free* tea. Many thanks to the enterprising Waltham Forest Club for this marvellous gesture.

All the time we had been overtaken by a gradually quickening stream of riders, big ones, little ones... all waved and cheered-and a toot on our exhaust whistle livened up the morning for most of them.

Perhaps now it is opportune to give a brief resume of Mr. John Marston's passenger outfit of 54 years ago. This motor bicycle (the Sunbeam was advertised as " The Gentleman's Motor Bicycle") was quite ahead of most of its contemporaries when it was announced in the summer of 1913.

LIKE its solo brethren, it has all-chain drive, handlebar clutch control, three-speed gearbox (the three-fifty had only two speeds) and twin oil baths for the chain to run in. The power unit in the ubiquitous 6.h.p (770 c.c) J.A.P. twin, side-valve of course. This engine, built by J.A. Prestwich of Tottenham, was used by many, if not most, makers for their sidecar models. It did not have the power of the 8 h.p (1000 c.c) model but seemed a more pleasant motor. I have driven similar engines in frames by Bat and Royal Enfield with, respectively, direct belt drive and two-speed chain drive and they both impressed me.

The Sunbeam is of course, finished in black. Not the original enamel but some as good, if not better, applied by my old friends, G. Smith Enamellers, 382 St. John Street, London. I know of nobody to equal the quality of their work, especially in respect for durability. Certainly there is no trace of rust coming through on the machines I rebuilt 10 years ago, whereas, with other concerns' work, I can already see craze lines though the job was done only two years ago- and the bike has not yet been assembled.

Matching the Sunbeam's finish is the Milford sidecar, made by Mills-Fulford of Coventry and rebuilt for me by Watsonian of Birmingham. Ah Watsonian; I recall another firm entering the sidecar market after the war and claiming to have most of it, but they don't make' em anymore. Watsonian's do. The Milford body is carried on Cee springs and has a sit-up position that makes it very comfortable. I'm told. It has a large wrap round celluloid screen and canvas apron which keeps out most of the weather but does not have a hood. A really splendid carrier is fitted to the back of the body, hence our ability to carry so much kit. The Sunbeam is completely reliable, especially since Stan Greening at J.A.P.'s (he's retired, they are no more) had some unbreakable valves turned up for me after a word on my behalf by Graham Walker. I remember listening to Graham on the phone to Stan in about 1955. "Ah, Stan. One of our chaps has a lot of trouble with breaking valves on his J.A.P. You'll make him some better ones? Good. Oh, it's a 1914 6 h.p. twin". He did, too, and they don't.

Of course, the Achilles heel of the outfit is the lack of brakes. The cycle-type front one is decorative, and the rear one acts like a dummy belt rim. One develops a kind of at-oneness with the outfit after a few miles and acquires a smoother, gentler driving techn-ique. If traffic lights came into view and are red, accelerate for they will be green by the time they are reached. If they show green, close the throttle and trickle along to let them turn full circle before reaching them! If the descent is steep, use middle gear to ensure adequate retardation.

Cruising at 30ish we were steadily covering the ground-as could be said of a variety of machinery that regularly passed us at 60-and then came by again (at 60) a few miles further on- and again and again-and often again!

It's a Zundapp- registered in this country.

TOO late I realised the odd bit of canvas on the opposite side of the road was a case of fishing rods. I did not notice a signpost pointing to Nocking but have yet to think up a clever use for it (hints welcome).

Other vintagents were few and far between. A big twin A.J.S. of about 1920 and a Raleigh of 1928 or 9 came by at Brownhills and a flat tank B.S.A. was parked at the roadside on the Shrewsbury by-pass, but no others were seen. Soon we crossed the border, an action that has been a cause of court action to many before, and so it proved on this occasion, for the police had a radar trap a *(seems like nothing has changed there then! a note from the author)* few miles further on- and a second one at Bet-See-Co-Ed.
(saves looking up the spelling).
Did anyone do the double?

Amid the trees of Glyn Padarn a city of multi-coloured tents springs up. Conditions were absolutely ideal.

There but for the pace of the Sunbeam went I. How lucky we didn't come on the McEvoy, with its thundering 8/45 o.h.v.J.A.P. and T.T. Hughes sidecar.....

At Capel Curig the tank was dry but I had a spare can on the carrier. Up the long climb, past the start of the Snowdon footpath and down, in second gear, to Llanberis. Sorry if I held you up on the descent-but those absent friends, brakes.....

Through the town and into the camp gates for the Rally is held at an old ammunition dump. Thoughtful officials directed me to hut 22, just inside-and found that the far corner of the far room was empty. Although never in the army, I recalled an army cadets camp and the advisability of walking over rather than been walked over.
I have always wanted to be nonchalant and I hope I was as Stephen and I unloaded the outfit while surrounded by the common market, represented by a quite uncommon herd.

I felt a lot better after a wash (the washroom was still passable) and, as with most ten-year-olds, Stephen felt much worse. We ate our lunch (it was 1.40 when we arrived, 150 miles in 6 hours 30 minutes) and then did a complete circumnavigation of the camp. Saw several foreign riders and bikes, a Zundapp flat-twin outfit with righthand sidecar and British plates, an impressive 250.c.c Empire Star B.S.A. of about 1938, several Broughs (I don't think G.B minds in the abbreviation now) and almost every S7 or S8 Sunbeam made. Filled in a form to say we might be eligible for the Vintage award- that was really why we came, of course- and decided to hang about at the gates and watch the later arrivals.

EVENTUALLY C.E.A. And F.P.M. and entourage arrived and, again trying my best to be nonchalant (I later gave it up for lent), I strolled over and asked if they had had trouble en route. I thought I noticed a flicker of surprise on C.E.A.'s face but it, too, went under another wave of nonchalance and I was regaled with tales of how son Roger's Golden Flash had sheared the fibre wheel on the auto advance-and how the new one cost more than the entire outfit. The cable and lever on my Sunbeam would cost all of 14s 2d. To replace if anyone pinched 'em..... it won't break, and I can fiddle with my own ignition, thank you.

C.E.A. pitched his tent, F.P.M. was awarded the C.D.M. for the dirtiest machine present, I discovered that a 1909 Triumph was present.

If you went to the Dragon Rally you don't need any long winded account of how the bonfire didn't light, how the crowd did sing, how the ghosts of Harley and Davidson winced at what had been done to their once proud motorcycles. Did you hear the appeal for a flywheel extractor for a Bantam-and then five minutes later, an appeal for the chap who wanted it to come and get it? Did you notice the wrecked "Dommie" in hut 22 and spare a thought for the one who didn't make it? Did you think that a bar was not really necessary? I enjoy a drink as much as most folk but I think the bar encourages too much drinking by many youngsters unused to it. Certainly we had one chap in our room who was sick on the hour, every hour, through the night. he woke us at 1.am, 2.am, 4.am, 5.am and 6.am., plus or minus five minutes, why?

If you didn't go to the Dragon, do so next year. You'll meet a surprising cross-section of people. The girl's voice in the dark that told the most vile stories, not funny either, belonged to quite a pleasant looking bird. The Welsh copper who enjoyed the Rally. "It's a dreary place here in winter". The chap who's Duggie arrived on one pot-and discovered that the other had cracked all round. It's an interesting experience and is different from any other event I've been to-and yet the same as them all. For, after all the essence of motorcycling is the nattering: no use doing the "ton" if you can't re-live it afterwards. I remember (dangerous beginning) Arthur Breese saying on the Golden Jubilee Lands End Trial (he was on a 350 c.c 1913 Sunbeam and I was on the "Dragon " oufit), " It's an event I shall enjoy in retrospect".

Sunday morning saw Stephen and me up at 7.am. We passed the kit through the window rather than try to negotiate the sleeping beauties, and after breakfast at the C.E.A. "caff" were away. We stopped for sausage, egg and chips in Llangollen (wonder if the Rocket rider and his wife got home safely to Birmingham), and then for tea with Waltham Forest Club, before arriving home at 3.00.pm to wash and change and work in the shop. C.E.A. and co. didn't catch us. Heard that a Norton had to be fetched on a trailer, later....And one chap on a Vincent solo-PAL were the registration letters-passed us at least three times. We averaged 20.m.p.h; I wonder what he will claim to have averaged when he writes to Motor Cycle Sport.

My thanks from us all to the stalwarts of the Conwy Club for organising us at Glyn Padarn, to the member of the Harley Davidson Club for amusing us all, and to all the people of Llanberis for putting up with us all. Next year? on second thoughts?

-J.G.

FROGMAN'S DRAGON

"There's snow on the mountains." That message passed down the A5 halts last Friday as the stream of riders poured into North Wales for the seventh Dragon Rally.

Weather conditions were perfect, too perfect. Snowdonia was bathed in the sharp, brittle sunshine of early spring. French rallyist Jean- Marie Debonneville made such good progress on his BMW outfit, he diverted to make a tour of North Wales, crossing Bwlch-y-Groes.

Another early arrival enjoying the sunshine was Donald Gross, who'd come all the way from Toronto, specially for the Dragon, on his Harley Davidson Servi-Car trike.

George Marren & Tom Sharkey manfully push their Arrow through the Nant Peris floods of 1968.

But winter suddenly sprang back with cruel talons. Squalls came sweeping in with nightfall. Icy rain turned to sleet and snow, and the authentic white stuff mantled the upper reaches of the A5.

Through the night riders had the roughest time. By the morning, the mountains were flecked white, not with snow but foaming torrents. Just as in 1966, the road flooded at Nant Peris. By noon, it needed a wary rider to keep his engine from drowning. At teatime, the water level of Llyn Peris had risen so high the police were forced to stop all traffic on the Llanberis Pass road.

Perhaps because many experienced Dragonists had assumed the six-weeks postponement would guarantee an easy ride, bookings had reached the comparatively modest figure of 2,500 (final tally was 3,330) How wrong we were!

"Hardest ride in 47 years motor cycling" declared Leo Starr who, at 67, took the award for the oldest entrant. He rode a Norton Atlas 290 miles from Gosport, too.

Six hardy types braved the Saturday afternoon freedom ride up the Snowdon miners' track. Bad though conditions were at Llanberis, in the 2,000ft-high cauldron of the Snowdon Horseshoe the wind reached hurricane force. Jean Sutton was plucked from her Triumph Trophy and sent sprawling.

This Dragon must have been the first at which not one solitary camp fire was lit for two days. Fortunately, the Conwy Club had been forewarned. Buried deeply beneath the bonfire pile lurked a scrapped Ford truck, keeping the paraffin-soaked kindling dry. When the first fire was struck, the bonfire leapt into a magnificent blaze.

With nightfall the storm redoubled its fury. Tents were literally torn to ribbons. A marquee collapsed entirely. Flooded out campers- *Motor Cycle's* staffman among them- scurried for shelter in draughty bunkers. In the small hours floods closed the Caernarvon road.The rally was cut off. Few were tempted to sleep late on Sunday. All over the Glyn Padarn site, rallyists wrung out saturated riding kit, or pushed and struggled to coax drowned ignition systems to spark. Dennis Baker of Stoke-on-Trent paused in his efforts with a Road Rocket to point to his 1968 Dragon badge. "When I flash this to the boys back home,"he growled , "I'll expect them to stand to attention and salute!"

by John Ebbrell

DRAGON STALWARTS WELCOME BLIZZARDS

It was the real hard core of enthusiastic motor cyclists who battled their way through the weekend's blizzards to take part in the annual Dragon Rally high in the Welsh mountains at Llanberis.

Almost 2000 of them, from as far afield as West Germany, Belgium and France fought their way through the worst conditions ever encountered during the eight years of the rally.

"As far as we were concerned it was the greatest Dragon ever," said Laurie Irving, secretary of the organising Conwy Club.

"Although it was the smallest attendance ever, we have reached the 6,000 mark, this weekend's events will go down as a vintage rally," he said. "Everyone was so enthusiastic and the atmosphere had everything this sort of rally should have."

Despite the conditions, the snow was lying a foot deep before drifting and the temperature was never much above freezing, new arrivals found plenty of help available as they cut through the snow to pitch their tents.

With the Llanberis Pass completely blocked by snow and unpassable for 12 hours many riders had to make the long detour along the A55 North Wales coast road to Bangor before heading inland.

One rider determined not to miss the Dragon because of a " little bit of snow," was 69 Year old Leo Starr who made the 630 mile round trip from Gosport in Hampshire. Leo, with seven TT replicas and 52 years of riding to his credit, arrived during Saturday Afternoon. This was a Dragon to remember.

Two outfits pulling a van up Pen y Pas. The road was blocked by the van until the rigs got it to the top.
Photos: Roger Newark

BRUCE POLLARD'S 1969 DRAGON RALLY

The first of many!

As a 16 year old I had a BSA C15 and my school friend Ian had a Triumph Tiger Cub, he told me about the Dragon Rally having read about it in the Motorcycle News. We decided to go, at that time I was living in Stourbridge in the West Midlands and whilst I had been camping in warm weather I had never camped in the winter or indeed gone any real distance on a motorcycle.

My mum cooked us a chicken to take with us and together with a packet of Smash (dried potatoes) and a tin of peas that was the food taken care of. Ian's dad, Major Taylor (he was a retired soldier having reached this rank at the end of the First World War) gave us each a 10 Shilling note to add to our meagre funds. I had some ex-Fireman leather boots and an ex-fire brigade jacket to wear. Crash helmets were worn to keep our heads warm although at that time they were not a legal requirement to wear.

Bruce Pollard in his younger days all ready and set to go to The Dragon Rally.

Saturday morning dawned; it had already snowed heavily but Ian came around on his bike and we decided to try to make it.

The roads were covered in snow and it was slow going, getting as far as Bridgnorth (14 miles) I fell off going around a bend, fortunately no damage was caused to me or the bike so onwards we went.

Further down the road a snow plough had cleared most of the snow. Eventually we reached Betws y Coed and stopped for beans on toast and a hot drink and continued onwards with both the road and the weather getting worse as we approached Llanberis Pass. On the way, in a blizzard, we passed a group of bikes by the roadside one of which I remember was belt driven, possibly a Triumph Single from the 1920,s. Going up the steep pass there was a hold-up caused by a coal lorry getting stuck.

We managed to get past and onwards we went. A mile or so over the top of the pass Ian's clutch gave trouble and we stopped alongside a broken down outfit with some Frenchmen on it, my schoolboy French was useless but a Welsh Special Constable assisted who could speak French. He arranged for assistance from the rally to fix the clutch and get the French Lad's outfit going, meanwhile we had a welcome cup of coffee in the Policeman's house.

Finally we got to the rally site in Llanberis which was held in an old RAF camp. The entry fee was, I think, 10 shillings. In we went together with a song sheet which I still have although I have managed to lose the badge and I would like to replace it.

RATHER then putting our Tent up we camped in a building which was described as the Generator House.

We then got our stove out and had chicken, potatoes and peas. After eating we two schoolboys went for a look around, there were hundreds, if not thousands, of motorcycles of all shapes and sizes, the majority being English made with a few Japanese bikes including a 750cc Honda 4 (the first one I'd seen).

We approached the bar but did not try to get a drink as we thought we would not be served as it was full of old men, that is men of at least 30 years old! Later we went to the Address of Welcome given by a Vicar followed by the Bonfire and a sing song. Returning to the Generator House, we talked with some other people and finally went to bed.

A cold night followed as the sleeping bags we had were not of a very good quality.

Sunday morning dawned and we had a hot drink and then got going again back home. The roads had by now improved and we stopped on the way back for a coffee.

Whilst parking outside the café an Ariel Square 4 went past at about 60mph towing a Vincent Twin, that was my Dream Bike in those days.

In addition we had seen in a lay-by a Nimbus, a 600cc Danish Bike. Nearing Bridgnorth again we stopped to talk to a bloke on a Greeves and as we had now no money left we managed to scrounge half a crown off him that is 12 ½ new pence and we had another coffee.

Bruce Pollard , a regular Dragon rallyist with his infamous Norton jumper!

A real eye opener for a young lad, I went again every year until 1977 then for reasons unknown did not go again until 1982 and since then I have managed to go every year and I am now one of the old men in the bar!

THE DRAGON OF DISCONTENT THE 1970S

The 1970s brought many changes to the Dragon. Managing the size of the numbers and keeping the taxman at bay caused rifts between the Conwy Club.

So Bomber, Laurence Irving, Tom Tiger and Kenny Davies took the initiative to go ahead with the rally and put their own money into the venture. Fortunately for them it was a success.

To keep the cost low the 1970 badge was a roundel with a bar and the 1971 badge was just a bar added on to the 1970s bar. Very similar to The Elephant Rally badges during these two years. The bars were unpopular so by 1973 the enamel badge, in all shapes and designs, was back and the Club had settled the rift. The Dragon was held at the popular site of Glyn Padarn for the last time in 1972.

1973 saw the new element to the Dragon Rally as a secret location. You sent for your ticket, then you were sent directions to a control point. Once you had exchanged your ticket for a pass into the rally site, you were given directions to the actual site. With many varied and sometimes extremely rural routes. This was done to stop the unruly element and from people arriving in cars. It worked, and the setup has lasted to this present day.

1974 became famously know as '*The Somme*' rally and was held at Tyn-Berth by Betws-y-Coed. After a week of rain many bikes got stuck in the mud of which in places was almost knee deep! It is well remembered by all who attended.

In 1975 the familiar site of Riverside near Capel Curig was used and became a popular venue over the years.

And then in the final years of the 1970s it moved to Twin Lakes, which was just up the road from the Riverside site. The Dragon then moved to Plas Irwg, up in the hills by Llanrwst for the last two rallies of the seventies.

In 1978 the first official Dragon sticker was produced, similar to the one pictured below.

A DRAGON IN THE HILLSIDE

Glad to be back in Llanberis. That was the decision of the 2,500 road riders who flocked to last weekend's tenth annual Dragon Rally in the heart of scenic Snowdonia.

But new organisers, the Dragon Rally Club, saw their first venture get off to a shaky start. By Saturday lunchtime only 1,000 had turned up at the disused ex-RAF site at Glyn Padarn. By early afternoon, however, convoys of as many as 20 machines at a time were converging on the lakeside village. In spite of the postal strike, total attendance was about 500 up on the last two years, with about 100 continentals making the chilly trek.

Local police were delighted with the orderly headlight procession in and around Llanberis on the Saturday night, but local pubs refused to open their doors in spite of a high standard of conduct from the Dragon enthusiasts.

With a £500 site rental sending overheads soaring, the Dragon Rally Club had to increase the entry fee to £1, but there were no complaints.

PC Graveson on his 750 Honda with Tokyo Police trim

Said Dutch Harley Davidson rider Wessel Ploeg: "This is the best rally in Europe-no cars at all. I'll be back again next year."Busy changing tyres on their 650 Triumph outfit-covers cost twice as much in France-Parisians Peter Palfalvi and Andre Laboulbene were in complete agreement.

They were attending their second Dragon-and looking forward to many more. Another foreigner enjoying himself was 27 -year-old Arne Polsen, who makes wooden legs for a living when back home in Oslo. He had journeyed from Norway via Newcastle -on-Tyne on his 1956 Jawa 175. "I help to organise the Troll Rally, so I can't really say this one is the best," he smiled.

After a short delay in badges arriving, 2,000 were scooped up inside three hours. Those who did not get badges will have to wait at least two months for them, says secretary Ken Davies.

Droitwich charioteer Brian Shore was one of 25 riders eligible for a special draw to win £25.00 worth of riding gear because he could produce all ten Dragon Rally badges since the event first took place. "The Dragon's a bit like the TT," he explained. "It's difficult to stop once you start going."

Furthest travelled rider was Sicilian Morisio Dasaro, whose solo BMW seized up in Paris after covering the 1,950 miles from his home town of Palermo. Undaunted Dasaro hitch-hiked from Paris to complete his journey to make his Dragon debut.

One of the main eye-catchers among the wealth of exotic machinery was a 750 Honda in Tokyo police trim, riden by constable Peter Graveson, a motor cycle instructor at Lancashire Constabulary's Preston driving school. Geared down for even hotter acceleration the bike sends the front wheel light just opening the throttle in fourth gear, reports PC Graveson. The bike is currently being tried out by several police forces.

Courtsey of The Motor Cycle News

TOUGH GOING IN SUNSHINE DRAGON

It looked like being an Easy Dragon Rally for southern riders as they set out on Friday afternoon. And it stayed that way in England. But, scarcely had competitors crossed the Welsh border than the rain came down in icy torrents and a headwind blew with hurricane force.

"We took as long to get from Llangollen to Llanberis as we did from Guildford to Llangollen," said Peter Gosdon, of Guildford, who had his wife on the pillion of his 650cc Matchless. They had braved the night crossing the Llanberis Pass to the Dragon site at Glyn Padarn; others had played safe.

A '59' Clubman's very lavishly decorated jacket.

Royal Enfield rider Norman Lloyd of Warwick, and his eight-year-old son Derek took shelter in a barn in Snowdonia. "It was so crowded with motor cyclists and climbers that even the cows couldn't get in. And the rain on the roof sounded like a non-stop express.

Daylight brought hail, like a million tiny icicles. Pat Brown of Leicester and his girlfriend Jo Stevens, trapped by a sudden squall in the wilds beyond Capel Curig, threw their Triumph down and dived for cover in the lee of a lay-by.

In the sheltered vale of Llanberis the weather was kinder and the move back to Glyn Padarn proved popular. When the control off-cially closed at noon on Sunday, 2,768 had booked in- the highest total since 1967.

This year's ad hoc organisers, The Dragon Rally Club, revived the popular headlight parade on Saturday night-and started it on time. Catering, long in adequate at earlier Dragons, was much better, with the commercial facilities, augmented by the Auto 66 Club's mobile canteen, and a barbeque laid on by the Trail Rider's fellowship and Panther Sidecar Club.

"Where shall we pitch our tent"? The perennial problem on the steep, slately slopes of the Glyn Padarn Dragon Rally site.

ORIGINAL PROGRAMME FROM THE 1971 DRAGON RALLY

10th ANNUAL DRAGON RALLY

PROGRAMME OF EVENTS

The Rally opens at 9 a.m. - 13th February. Soup, badges available etc.

Film show - From 1 p.m. until 8 p.m.
Films by courtesy of Castrol Ltd.

Bar opens at 6 p.m.

Night run to assemble at 6.30 p.m. for the start at 7 p.m.

Soup served all day until 7.30 p.m.

Address of Welcome - 7.30 p.m.

Lighting of the Bonfire - 7.45 p.m.

Sing song around the bonfire 8 p.m.

Bar to close at 11 p.m.

Rally control closes at 11 a.m. on Sunday 14th February.

PLEASE USE DUCKHAMS BAGS FOR LITTER

CHAIRMAN'S LETTER

A Hearty and warm welcome to this our 10th ANNUAL DRAGON RALLY - indeed, the Rally that nearly 'Never Was'- this being due to site problems and the venue in general - but here we are once again, problems overcome, among the mountains of Wales and back in the 'Old Routine', with old and new friends gathering together come snow, hail, rain or shine, on this pilgrimage that is our yearly MUST.

Entries have of course been slowed down through the postal strike - but, as we can see, this has made no great difference, as the enthusiasts have arrived at the gate per usual. It is heartening to see peoples that have come along to this rally, making the attendance of nine and ten to their credit...... 'If anyone can produce the ten rally badges to prove that they have attended all of the rallies, we are giving away prizes such as - A complete Motor Cycle suit, Twelve months free subscription to the Motor Cycling, Duckham's Oil etc. Claims can be made for these prizes at the caravan over the week end ....How many are there of you, that can claim to be these Veterans - GOOD LUCK.

Llanberis, is we feel an ideal site for the Dragon Rally a good place to get to and taking in some lovely scenery en route. The villagers welcome having us here for this week end, but we do ask you to pay respect to the town in general, such as keeping noise down, and not taking your machines out of the camp after 6 p.m. It's not far to walk!!! and if you like to have a drink as most of us do, the hotels will welcome your business, but not breadages to windows etc:

The camp site is primative we know, but of course we all love this at heart - may we ask you to use the rubbish bins provided, or put your week-end tins etc. in neat heaps for us to gather after the rally, think of our backs bending every time we pick up the leftovers!! MANY THANKS

DRAGON RALLY 'STARR'

If anyone had any doubts about the value of this year's Dragon Rally, following fears that the annual gathering might be terminated, Leo Starr, winner of the oldest participant award and a sprightly 71-year-old, would soon put them right.

" I nearly didn't make it," he exclaimed, " I've survived seven severe heart attacks over the last year, but I met a friend here who I haven't seen for over 20 years- it's amazing."

Seventy-one-year old Leo Starr, former TT rider (right), shakes hands with the man he hadn't seen for over twenty years Dennis Heap from Crewe.

His friend, Dennis Heap from Crewe, had been similarly surprised. " I thought to myself, that looks like Leo, and it was-incredible. Do you know the last time we met, over twenty years ago, I had a 46 BSA B31 and Leo, who was racing, had a Gold Star."

Now both men ride foreign, Leo a 450 Honda and Dennis a BMW R50.

Born in 1962 the Dragon has been suffering from people intent on causing trouble. This year at Llanberis has been no exception, and it can only be hoped that the organisers decide to operate a form of ticket only event next year and issue tickets to bonafide clubs only. Maybe then, the undesirable element can be replaced by those who stay away because of it. Luckily, disturbances were confined to the camp site, possibly because only one pub stayed open in the town.

The Dragon Rally started life in good form, but is beginning to get a little too weary. It must be time either to kill the beast stone dead or take steps to control some of the participants who seem bent on stabbing the Dragon, and motorcycling in general, in the back.

However the event held for many, like myself included, the pleasure of meeting old buddies and make some new ones.

One couple who experienced something of the true spirit of rallyists were Mick and Carol Watson from Andover, who had plug cap bothers on their new Honda. Steady drizzle played havoc with the original metal Honda units, and by the time these were replaced, it was late Friday night, and they were stuck in Shrewsbury. " If you are looking for somewhere to stay," a passer-by remarked, "there are some motorcyclists living down there."

The instructions led them to the doorstop of Trevor and Dot McGiven's home where they were made more than welcome.

In the morning, they went down to breakfast and discovered that they weren't the only guests. Trevor and Dot had some German friends over for the Dragon.....

At Llanberis on Saturday night, the usual attractions were laid on. The headlight parade, the discotheque, the massive bonfire, the night ride. The last event caused a few chuckles when one of the Liverpool lads remarked that they'd be putting out a call for a tow rope soon. He mimicked the PA system quite well and assured all that "it never fails-some blighter gets 'ere and then breaks down on the night ride." Sure enough the next announcement over the PA was........

WHILE the rally organisers provided some sideshows, the main interest of most people was to wonder at the machinery, like the furthest travelled, by 38-year-old West German Eberhard Lubke Munch-4-bigger in the flesh than 100 photographs could ever show.

Characters too gave rise to some comment, or rather their clothing did. Johnny Emms from Reditch-a professional singer and pianist-wore a jacket covered in badges that he valued at about £25.00. The jacket itself cost seven pounds.

On Sunday morning, some early birds managed to get a wash before the water was cut off and supplies could not be restored.

And so the 1972 Dragon Rally came to a close with the smoke haze of so many bonfires hanging in the valley like a great question mark hovering over the future of the event.

Footnote: The 380 Suzuki three cylinder machine that took me to the Dragon Rally and back home, behaved perfectly. It managed to cause quite a bit of confusion while parked at the rally, for with four silencer/expansion chambers displayed at the rear, many rallyists mistook it for a 750-4 or a 350-4. If anyone had bets on the bike being either of these. I'm sorry, you lost!

Sidecars on parade as the Welsh village of Llanberis fills up with bikes during this years Dragon. Photograph by Ray Daniel

Written By Jerry Clayton

An Ural Mars piloted by British importer Fred Wells, passenger in the middle of front row is Russian Boris Kusmin. The first Russian to attend the Dragon Rally.

Award a big E for effort to Frenchman Georges Fleutiaux. He rode 825 miles to the weekend's Dragon Rally, In North Wales, and spent just 50 minutes at Britains most famous winter get-together before starting on the return journey!

A train driver, Fleutiaux worked all Thursday night to earn a Friday holiday, and set off from his home in La Rochelle on the Bay of Biscay as soon as his shift had finished.

Riding an R75/5 BMW he splashed through over 300 miles of rain to the Le Harve-Southampton ferry, then pushed on non-stop through Britain to arrive at the Llanberis venue at 4.00pm on Saturday. And at 4.50pm exactly, the Frenchman started out on the long ride back home-for he explained, he must be on duty Monday morning! Fleutiaux considered his brief stay well worth the journey. " I had only 40 minutes at the Troll Rally In Norway. The enthusiasm here is incredible." He did not even stay long enough formally to stake his claim to the long distance award. And that 825 mile haul from La Rochelle would have put him exactly four miles ahead of the declared winner- Munch Mammut soloist Eberhard Lubke.

THE DRAGON FIGHTS TO STAY ALIVE

Although late starters enjoyed clear weather with only the occasional squall over Snowdon, early birds had to brave icy rain and driving sleet through Friday night.

I broke off a trail-riding trip to the Berwyn Mountains to ride to the Dragon, and early on Saturday morning the 1,850ft-plus summit of Wayfarer's Track was sheeted ankle-deep in fresh fallen snow.

Blackpool Men Paul Lewis and friends. In the background English rallyists puzzle over the insignia daubed on the wall-it belongs to the Free Wales Army.

At Glyn Padarn, old timers sighed about the large proportion of chopper-borne rallyists and their inevitable lurid attire. " Two piece riding suit, good; denim jacket with the sleeves torn off, bad, groaned one veteran, but any fears of wild behaviour were proved groundless.

Organisation in the hands of the Dragon Sporting Club an offshoot of the Conwy Club was exceptionally good-backed up by the discreet presence of the Gwynedd police. Rally attendance was slightly down on last year's with a head count of 2,108.

All the old favourites-headlight parade, bonfire, sing-song-featured in the programme, with this years discotheque on the Saturday night and in the afternoon, a standard machine trial in the slate quarries above the campsite. To clean the taped sections demanded a cross-country bike and riding skill of fair order, as London dealer Fred Wells soon discovered when he rolled up to try his luck with one of his mighty Russian flat-twin outfits.

After the 1971 Dragon, the Conwy Club made a painstaking search for rallyists with all ten of the coveted badges since the junket began in 1962. Twelve months research among many thousands of names turned up 21 riders. Each of them will shortly receive a souvenir tankard from the Dragon Sporting Club to mark the decade.

With snow-flecked mountains on all sides, rallyists head through the Llanberis Pass.

AWARDS

Farthest travelled Rider. overall.
E. Lubke, Oldenburg, W Germany, 821 miles.
Great Britain: R. Chapman and L. Rutter (jointly)., both from Falmouth,415 miles.
Woman: Mrs. Ann Barton, Darenth, Kent 290 miles.

Pre-1937 Machines, Age/Mileage
P. Rose (1936 BSA). Hounslow, Middx, 260 miles

Best Percentage Club Turn-out:
Wyvern Touring, Bideford, Devon, five riders 71 %.

Oldest rider: L. Starr, Gosport, 71.

HAVOC IS A DRAGON TRAPPED IN MUD!

Unprecedented rainfall played havoc with the 13th Dragon Rally held on farmland at Tyn-y-Berth, near Betws-y-Coed, Caernarvonshire, last weekend. Organising Conwy Club stalwart Don Williams said , " Its just one of those rare things. Three weeks ago, Caernarvon reservoir was so low they were talking about water rationing. Since then, we have had three months supply of rain and the campsite looks like a battlefield on the Somme!"

During Saturday, things became so bad that many rallyists arrived at the gate, parked their machines in the roadway and squelched their way on foot to the soup tent to collect badges before returning straight back home. Slightly overwhelmed by the catastrophic conditions, the Conwy Club forgot their usual selection of pop music on the PA system, and apart from the occasional wisecracking announcement it was up to the participants to entertain themselves.

The Somme-Dragon Style. Many a brave heart fluttered in this lot and many rallyists aimed at getting their machines clear before bringing out baggage & tent, here Conwy Club members help out with a rope.

I arrived in the dark on Saturday and attempted to get the 350 Jawa into the field. Like so many others, when all traction disappeared, I started to push through mud that was over the wheel rims. Within seconds, three others were pushing the Jawa towards terra firma. Whoever you were in the moment of blood, sweat and tears..... thanks!

For my own tent-pitching spot of dry land I'm indebted to Mike Muir from Crawley in Sussex, "There's a space next to my tent mate" and his friends Keith Mountain, Andrew Wynn and Tony Holland.

As if the weather hadn't done enough, some wag (for want of a stronger word) had tampered with the signposting of the route to the rally site and several of us spent a fruitless half hour zooming blindly up dead end forestry tracks. Still some people make life difficult in other ways. Three employees of Velo Solex GB took two Solex mopeds to the rally. Fifteen stone workshop manager Terry Mears rode one and Colin Slaney the other, while Steve Carroll rode shotgun on a scooter that carried a spare moped engine on the rear carrier. The tiny machines, unusual with shift drive and rear cable operated disc brakes had covered 250 miles to reach the rally and were still going strong when passed on the return journey near Froncysyllte.

Steve Carroll (17) and Colin Slaney (22) pose with the Solex mopeds that covered 250 miles to reach the Dragon.

The Dragon site looked like a battlefield, and typically, British humour shone through all the adversity. The floor of the soup tent was in almost the same state as the morass outside and as I stepped through the flap, a voice boomed, " Oi, wipe your feet!"

By Jerry Clayton

THE BLOODY MUDDY LIMIT

"Is this really the Dragon Rally? I hadn't bargained for a treasure hunt and trail ride," groaned David Russell as he and Steve Taylor tried to extricate their heavily loaded 650cc BSA sidecar outfit, wedged in an overgrown track miles from anywhere in North Wales on Saturday. And this was fervently echoed by the rest of the 1,329 Dragonists.

For Conwy Club, determined not to allow the unseasonably mild winter make Britain's oldest and traditionally most spartan rally too easy, obliged with a complex 10 mile closing route over mountainous forestry roads that would have done credit to a long-distance trail.

A Steib Chart attached to a BSA A7 or A10 stuck in the mud leaving the Dragon. Photo by Bruce Pollard.

Following the successful lead given by the 1973 Dragon, this years event again used a "secret" site, the exact location of which-four miles south-west of Betws-y-Coed was vouchsafed to entrants only when they checked in at a forwarding control. This double-checked against gatecrashing by hoodlums worked beyond the organisers wildest dreams.

A beat-up ford saloon, crammed with half a dozen visitors, was turned away by the control and tried tailing rallyists to the site until it became horribly wedged (to everyone's glee) on the wild track through Gwydyr Forest. In fact, the Conwy Club's plot worked so well that a fair number of experienced Dragonists spent hours finding the forwarding control and even longer playing hunt-the-rally-site. Some heavy machines, unwieldy with piled camping gear, jibbed at the shale-surfaced 1-in-6 gradients of Gwydyr and their riders vainly sought to loop round by tarmac roads.

For the site, Ty'-ny-Berth ("Beautiful small holding") tucked away on the south shore of the Lledr River, was completely new to the Dragon Rally. This spot is little visited even by the tourists who know North Wales well, and the forwarding control was equally obscure almost 1,600ft up, in the wild moorland west of Ffestiniog. Add control location directions which many folk found somewhat ambiguous, and route direction signs turned by rustic practical jokers, and hundreds of Dragonists had the perfect recipe for a magical mystery tour! However some experienced rallyists made the most of this new terrain and beautiful scenery in Wales. Control directions began at Bala, well away from the long-familiar A5, so Tony Luker of Abingdon, who boasts he's missed only one Dragon out of all 13, rode his BSA to the Welsh town along the remote B-road over the Berwyn Mountains.

The weather, was in the best Dragon tradition-appalling. It poured down all day on Friday and from dawn on Saturday morning. Indeed, snow flecked the Berwyns, but the only rider who reported being held up by the white stuff was Andrew Airey (350 Ariel) whose home,at the top of a one-in-five hill in Stalybridge, Cheshire, was virtually marooned by a glissade when he tried to leave at breakfast-time on Friday.

THE BLOODY MUDDY LIMIT

We got back last night from a holiday in Cairo, " WIMA stalwart Maureen Willis called from her Honda as icy rain lashed almost horizontally across the Ffestiniog moors. "Two days ago I was riding a camel through 80 degrees in the shade. What a difference."

Only from Ireland (of all places), did rallyists report dry roads.

Unfortunately low-lying Ty'n-y-Berth soon looked like a mud bath. Despite digging drainage ditches, the Conwy Club were shocked to see how swiftly 3,000 churning wheels turned wet grass into an ankle deep quagmire. Swiftly they dismantled the bonfire to produce a makeshift "corduroy" pathway, but it made little difference.

In Betws-y-Coed every Hotel and guesthouse in the picturesque village was crammed full.

Late on Saturday afternoon the rain turned into a driving torrent. The soup kitchen and burger stand marquee were swiftly packed with rallyists enjoying that never-failing Dragon pastime, swapping lurid tales and keeping dry.

Eventually, under leaden skies the now rebuilt traditional bonfire made a cheery blaze to hearten soggy spirits. There was water a-plenty, but this years Dragon was again "dry", and to find stronger liquor meant a three mile hike to the nearest pub (for once on the site, it was virtually impossible to ride off it again). Thirsty Dragonists drudged up to the Waterloo Hotel by the famous iron bridge over the river Conwy, but the local people rose to the occasion. Soon, a bar which overflowed with folk across the car park was bawling out the famous rugby choruses.

After such a lengthy return trip, they were unusually sober and footsore Dragonists who thankfully crawled into their sodden sleeping bags. Through the small hours of Sunday a relentless downpour thundered down, until the roaring torrent of the Lledr seemed as though it would burst its banks and wash the entire rally down to Conwy town. The hesitant sun rose on a scene out of World War One. What was once green had long since been churned to brown. Mud encrusted figures cursed reluctant stoves, and reeled like drunkards as they lurched back from water points, pushed, stumbled and fell behind flailing bikes. Observed Frenchman Marc Boselli, for the second year running winner of the farthest travelled award, *"C'est comme la grande bataille de Verdun!"*

Mutterd Englishman Peter Symes, falling flat on his face behind Barry Noakes' wallowing Honda, "This is the bloody, muddy limit!"

AWARDS

Farthest- travelled rider: *Overall M. Boselli (750 Honda sc) Metz, France, 690 miles.*
Great Britan, R.L Barry (BMW R75/5), Lossiemouth, 505 miles
Woman, Mrs G. M.Russell de Clifford (250 Honda), Bournemouth, 280 miles.
Veteran machine: *P . Bickerstaff (1937 500 Vincent-HRD sc), Glastonbury, 200 miles.*
Best Club: *Newport MCC, Salop (96 per cent turnout)*

Written by John Ebbrell

A DRY DRAGON 1975

Nine hours of grim riding on a machine meant for short commuter hops, with a maximum speed of 30 mph and, more often than is good for the human body, a hard slog of pedalling uphills- that's what won the award for the most eventful journey in last weekend's Dragon Rally.

A badly worded title really, for there's not many exciting things that can happen in over a 100 miles of riding a 49cc Raleigh moped. But this didn't deter Mr Francis, the intrepid voyager, from starting off back home to Birmingham from the campsite five miles west from Betws-y-Coed, after just fourteen hours rest.

But at least he had good weather, clear blue skies greeted arrivals on Saturday, and, though very cold and frosty, saw off nearly 2,000 departing rallyists on Sunday morning. A complete and welcome change from the torrential rain of recent years.

Also a change from last year, the campsite, well organised and laid out, was easy to find. The organising Conwy Club again employed their system of a control point forwarding on genuine enthusiasts. This idea, to avoid visits from vandals-five years ago-they lost there regular site-worked well with few complaints.

Anyone who has never been to the Dragon may wonder what possesses so many happy souls to ride a couple of hundred miles in usually poor weather, just to camp in a field which may or may not be awash. The main justification is the friendliness and comradeship that exists wherever you get a gathering of bikers.

This intangible bond is apparent in many ways. Like the appeals over the tannoy for help and/or spares. Calls were made for welding gear (supplied by the local garage), spare handlebars, Triumph spares in general, oils and even a timing chain for a BSA A10- most, if not all of these cries were satisfied.

Chris Beesley, from Cheadle, Staffs, presented his problem to the control caravan-a minute crack in the handlebars of his Ariel VB outfit had yawned dangerously and was only noticed on Sunday morning. Chris, who came with nine others of the Market Drayton MC, eventually left with instructions to contact a local garage mechanic who'd weld the break. Proof of the popularity of the rally came with the arrival of three sets of Continentals- six Germans, three Dutch and six French. The French riders, didn't arrive until well after dusk but were up and packed to leave by eleven the next morning.

Competing with Mr Francis for the most eventful journey award was G.D. Sherry who rode a 650 cc Triumph from Ellesmere in Salop, riding over 90 miles-with a broken left arm. His comment was, "I was only able to use the clutch when I threw my arm at it and managed to catch it!"

Only injury reported was when Ron Barber of Rainham Essex, slid his bike into a hedge on the road near Bala. Ron was only shaken, but his son, who was riding pillion, broke a wrist and spent the day in Wrexham hospital. It was a new bike too!

After arriving at the site, rallyists reported to the check-in for their badge and were greeted by the customary welcome cup of soup. For those who fancied themselves as a lampkin, there was a mini trials course laid out over rocks, bogs and puddles. A contest for production bikes was won by P. Barnfield from Oswestry, Salop, on a 250 cc BSA.

COLD SNAP OF THE DRAGON

For the first time since the 1960s, the Dragon Rally was completely free from the rowdy element which had spoilt it in the past.

The system of rallyists having to go to a designated check-point- introduced five years ago- before being told the exact location of the site seems to achieved its aim. The result last weekend was one of the quietest rallies on record.

The organising Conwy Club's treasurer Dave Williams said, " It was one of the smoothest Dragons we have ever had. The system certainly had its desired effect, although it can be unfair. By limiting the numbers to 1,500 this year meant that about 400 applicants had to be turned down. The 1,500 limit was reached three days after advertising the rally, so we probably had to turn away people who had been to virtually every rally. A suggestion has been made to introduce a new system whereby people can only join the rally if they are introduced by someone we know. To see exactly what the rallyists themselves want, we have issued a questionnaire, with various suggestions, including this one, for future rallies."

This years site was situated directly between the North Wales village of Capel Curig and Mount Snowdon, in the bleak and open Dyffryn Mynbyr valley, at Garth Farm.

The valley is noted for biting cold winds and some climbers have died of exposure there in the past, but most rallyists took heed of the warnings and came prepared for the worst weather. One or two did not, however, and one collapsed with cold on Sunday morning.

Traditionally, the weather stayed very wet, and cold and on Sunday morning, the rain turned to a heavy fall of snow.

Perhaps the Conwy Club's lead in avoiding rally rowdyism could be followed at the Elephant Rally, which was spoiled by trouble, culminating in a rallyist being shot dead by police earlier this month.

Harold Claus and Minimax Paul, who rode their 750 BMW outfit 1,000 miles across Germany and Holland to be at the Dragon, said strong rumours in Germany suggested that the Elephant's organising club was on the verge of folding up, and it was touch and go as to whether there would be any more rallies at Nurburgring.

This year's rally has been the final straw. The two Germans picked up the Dragons furthest travelled award.

Part of the rally site on Sunday morning, when the snow came down in a blizzard to really make the 1977 a Dragon to remember.

COLD SNAP AT THE DRAGON

Unlucky not to pick up on the long distance award was Paul Smaja, who travelled 600 miles from Paris on a 125 cc Honda for his second visit to the Dragon. He only bought the bike the previous Monday, specially for the rally, and is planning to get a Norton Commando for the next year's Dragon. He travelled part of the way with Herve Le Manach and Herve Hanon, who rode a 500 cc AJS single cylinder outfit from Brittany. They also have other British machines-Herve Hanon is the only French member of the Rudge Owners Club, and Herve Le Manach has two Panthers.

With his 600 BMW tucked away in his garage, Alan Roberts from Grange Farm Motor Cycle Club again rode his 150 MZ the 200 miles to the Dragon. He originally bought the bike for short trips around town, but now uses it solely for rallies, and has carried Alan to three Dragons and two Elephants.

Terry Chapman from Boreham Wood, London, stripped and cleaned the magneto and carbs on his T110 Triton after it failed to restart when he arrived at the site. There was plenty of spark and ample petrol, but the Triumph refused to fire until the following morning. Rumour has it that Terry frightened the engine into life with the most essential part of the Triumph tool kit - a big hammer! Terry's old bike, also a big Triumph, started first kick every time for his friend Richard King, who also rode up from London.

Time to head for home, and these three Frenchman have a long, cold and wet journey to Paris ahead of them.

Problems also plagued Barry Lewis, from Camberley in Surrey, on his Kawasaki Z400, his speedometer broke as he left his house, followed by the rear light and indicator bulbs blowing, then the head gasket blew, the engine sprang a load of oil leaks and the rear tyre punctured twice.

In conclusion I must mention four rallyists who hitched a lift from the site to the nearest pub. They literally tried to 'bum' a lift by crouching at the side of the road with their trousers round their ankles. I bet that cold night wind brought a glow to their cheeks!

By Ron Pearson
Courtesy of Motor Cycle News

AWARDS

Club Award: Ravens Motor Cycle Club from Prestatyn with 38 members.
Best Special: Mick Bartlett's BSA Austin Cooper.
Vintage: Kevin Earley from Uttoxeter, Velocette 250 MOV of 1939.
Furthest Travelled: Harold Claus and Minimax Paul from Wuppertal, West Germany-1,000 miles on a 750 BMW outfit.
Furthest Travelled Lady Rider: Mrs. Mary Russel de Clifford from Bournemouth, Dorset, 409 miles on a 550 Honda Four.

DRAGON RALLY COASTERS FROM 1997-2010

There was no 2008 coaster produced for the Dragon Rally

DRAGON RALLY BADGES 1962-1986

DRAGON RALLY BADGES 1987 -2010

THE DRAGON REACHES ITS 25TH ANNIVERSARY

During the 1980s most of the Dragon Rallies were held at the Riverside site near Capel Curig. With exceptions of Bettws Garmon, 1980, Pentir near Bangor, 1984, Nant Gwynant near Beddgelert, 1998 and the famous 1985 Dragon held for the last time at Gwyrch Castle. The 1985 Dragon was snow bound and not many rallyists got through to it. Roughly only about 600 made it to Gwyrch Castle. And well over half of these were sidecarists.

So in the early spring a mini rally was held at the Pondarosa Cafe on the Horseshoe Pass for the Dragonists who were unable to attend the original rally in February, due to the adverse weather conditions. When they received their badges the date was grounded off. The badge below is an original.

Dave Pearson's photo at the Pondarosa Cafe for the Dragon rallyists in early spring of 1985.

But the following year the Dragon Rally celebrated its 25th Anniversary, which many thought it would never make it past the first decade let alone more than two. But the Conwy Club and Dragon Rallyists proved to show many Motor Cycle Magazines and critics that it was here to stay. This was the year when they produced the Dragon woolly hat, shown below.

DRAGON TAKES A BATH

While I was wallowing in the mud at the Black Friar's Mad Monks Rally, POC supremo, Steve Rogers *MA Cantab*, was doing the same thing at the Conwy Clubs Dragon Rally. My thanks to Steve for this report and pictures.......

It was wet this year at the Dragon-so wet that the traditional bonfire was, at times, in danger of going out and rallyists, standing up to their ankles in mud and water, had to lean against it to feel any warmth.

This year 456 hardy souls attended the Dragon, ironically held in the shadow of a mountain known locally because of its shape as an Elephant! Near constant rain during the preceding week had left roads flooded and the site - this year an official campsite with real toilets! - ready to be converted into a mudbath - and so it was!

And of course, from the legions of Panthers ranging from 1927 to 1964, by far the most fascinating machine there was a Honda 50 combination - no, that is not a misprint! owned by Mike Donovan of Limerick, which deservedly won the Best Special award. Based on a stripped down "step through", Mike claimed that it did 40mph two up. As he said: "It's something different!"

The Long Distance award went to Alain Lagarrique, who with his companion, Genevieve Lapate, who won the Long Distance female award, had come 1,030 miles from Montpelier, France, on their SR and XT 500 Yamahas. There's nothing like a big single even if it is made on the wrong side of the world.

Most Distant entrant award went to John Williams from Auckland in New Zealand, who was over here on a working holiday.

Best Vintage Machine award went to Pete Bickerstaff who had come 200 miles from Glastonbury on his 1926 500 HRD and club turnout award went to the Fox and Duck, Walcott club from Shropshire who had 23 out of their 44 members there.

Conwy Club chairman, Bryn Thomas was full of praise for the hard work of the 30 members of the club who had helped organise the rally and also for 8 year old Tray Rimmer of the 8th Hayes club pack, Middlesex, who while his father slept, helped the Conwy Club sweeping, clearing up, keeping the fire going, in fact anything he was asked to do-a future club organiser obviously!

The mighty Panther Owners Club had a fine turnout of about 20 members to give the Dragon a bit of class.

Written by Steve Rogers

A group of Dragon rallyists enjoying the brief winter sunshine at the 1980 Dragon rally.

STATE OF THE ART DRAGON RALLY, OR AN INDUSTRY?

I like the Dragon Rally; I've been seven times- which is nothing compared with people like the Kettle brothers, Tony Luker and Dennis Jones, the only riders to have done all 20 Dragon Rallies. But it's still enough for me to know that I like it. This year it was held at Capel Curig.

I've also spent a lot of time over the past few years exhorting other motor cyclists to go, particularly the Panther Owners Club where it has become a tradition to set off for Snowdonia in February. Ahh.... Snowdonia in February-there's the nub! Crisp air, beautiful scenery, swooping through the bends - oh yes, you can swoop on a Panther with Busmar double adult; it's just a different sort of swooping- and even some snow if you are lucky.

One club that's bound to think the Dragon entry fee worthwhile is the Fox and Duck- they took the club turnout.

But I probably won't go next year. The Dragon has always been a traditional rally. Soup when you get there, bonfire and badge, the bare essentials. It doesn't need anything else; the fact that it's the Dragon, it's in Snowdonia and there is more than 1,500 motor cyclists there is enough. But you cannot tell ne that inflation affects such a rally at the rate of 100 per cent a year! To be fair Conwy Club, they did provide a sort of food parcel this year (**The food parcel - an essential part of the rally in my book, especially the whisky! authors note)* of chocolate, instant snack and a miniature bottle of whisky and estimated that they paid back £2 out of the £5 in goodies.

But with 1,350 minimum attending the rally this year leaves £4,500 to pay for the badge, field etc.

Secretary Graham Bradshaw denied that the Conwy Club was the most wealthy motor cycle club in the world - pointing out that as they run two scrambles and five motor cycle shows during the year they have to pay 40 per cent back in tax. I must admit that I was a little confused by that, but unfortunately their treasurer wasn't around to comment.

Perhaps I'm naive but I would of thought that the bigger the rally the cheaper it should run - it being more cost effective.

Even without the snow the Dragon offers some of the best scenery in the Country.

There is also the law of supply and demand - ie, the more people who want to go the more you can charge.

If the Conwy Club can charge £5 this year and get away with it, why not £10 next year?

There will always be some mugs who will pay it and it would have the added advantage of making the same amount of money out of half as many people- thus less problems in organisation.

1981 DRAGON CONTINUED

I think the Dragon Rally should not become a money spinner. It is the oldest and most famous of British rallies and something of a national institution.

This year many people did not go because they objected to the price rise - one rider who had attended all 19 previous rallies wrote in to say as much, and many who were there said that this would probably be their last Dragon.

There were even mumblings among the Panther Owners Club about organising our own private Snowdonia winter camping weekend on the same weekend as the Dragon next year.

Next year is the 21st Dragon Rally and the Conwy Club promise grand things. With the profit from this year they should be able to afford it.

Written by Steve Rogers of the Panthers Owners Club for MCW

I found the Dragon Rally enjoyable and met some great people and saw some great bikes. However, may I make what I hope is a couple of constructive criticisms.

On the information sheet, sent with the tickets, would it be possible to state at what time and on which day the control caravan is open? many riders, myself included, didn't realise that the Dragon Rally was only a two day event. This would have been obvious had the relevant times been included on the information sheet.

While I appreciate that a certain amount of secrecy is necessary to preserve the rally site from unwanted elements, would it be possible to improve the sign posting to the site? I had cause to stand by the roadside at the turn-off to the camp site, and direct many people who had missed the road the first time around, on to the right road.

These points are in no way intended to be negative, quite the reverse, it was a good rally despite the problems.

I shall certainly go again and recommend anyone to make the effort.

Sent into the Motor Cycle Weekly by Mark Reynolds, Alton, Hants.

THE DRAGON CELEBRATES ITS 21ST ANNIVERSARY

The Dragon Celebrated its 21st year at the weekend-but there was no special birthday party for the 1,300 riders who made the pilgrimage to Britain's best-known rally.

"It's a pity," said Conwy and District M.C.C chairman Dave Wainwright, "but even a special badge would have cost us so much more that we would have had to put the price above £5.

"We have been accused of high fees-and we reckoned anything above £5 for a ticket would be too much."

A Welsh river valley becomes hazy with wood smoke while a thousand Motor cyclists prepare for a ride home.

For this coming-of-age year, the Dragon Rally returned to a riverside site near Capel Curig, last used in 1976.

In line with the club's policy that riders should bring what you'll need only-a marquee, toilets and burger van were on site for the traditional-style-event. It looked as if the organising might have been washed out when a steady downpour hampered the clubmen on Friday. luckily, a good access road prevented the rally turning into a mud bath over the weekend.

Attendance was down on last years total and there was noticeable absence of continental riders. It looked as though many faced with a long distance ride had thought twice about a wet weekend in Wales. But the hard core of Dragon regulars couldn't be put off. No less than a dozen riders who had been every year- or very nearly- gathered to talk about old times.

" It is some kind of achievement to have done 21 years of rallying." reflected Dave Wainwright. The Rally has been an apprenticeship to motor cycling experiences given to thousands of riders over the years."

Despite the big crowd, there were no complaints from two local pubs which were swamped by riders looking for a pint in the dry-and the local police kept a low profile.

No doubt many riders, like me, thought it was all worthwhile just to spend a sunny Sunday taking the scenic route home.

The old timers line-up (left to right):Glenys Thomas, Ken Davies, Bomber Thomas, John Chamberlain, Alan Roberts, Alwyn Kettle, Husband and wife Maurice & Freda Kettle (21 badges!) With Tony Luker, Dennis Walker, Haydn Rees, John Redford and Brian Watson.

AWARDS

Furthest travelled rider: Mr I.D Winnan, Falmouth, Cornwall.

Most Distant male rider: Paul Minimax Hoppe, Wupperthal, West Germany.

Most Distant female rider: Linda Brown, Headington, Oxford.

Best Special: Tim Box's Tribsa.

Best Vintage: Dick Powell's 1938 Ariel 250 (11 hours on the road from Braunton, Devon.)

Best Outfit: M.C Reynolds Gold Wing, Kent.

Club Award: The Hundred Club, based at the Grey-Hound, Eldersfield, Nr Gloucester. (179 miles with 13 out of 14 present)

By Terry Snelling

A WELCOMING DRAGON IN THE HILLSIDES

More than 1,500 bikers wound their way through the Welsh mountains on Saturday for Britain'oldest rally, the Dragon.

With surprisingly mild weather, many decided to travel hundreds of miles on the off-chance of picking up a ticket along the way. One such stalwart was regular Dragonist George Theissen, who drove his Moto Guzzi 500 single from Luxembourg and finally managed to buy a spare ticket from bikers he met on the A1.

Getting a lift to the Dragon on Dave's Bonnie Tourer. Photo by Dave Pearson.

Many riders only attend one rally a year- the Dragon. Which began 22 years ago in response to the already successful Elephant Rally on the Continent.

At first, 5,000 riders braved the winter's blast to attend, but this unwieldy number has since been whittled by the organisers, Conwy and District M.C.C.

Club secretary, Graham Bradshaw said: " About half the riders who came ride several hundred miles regardless of the weather." So why do these apparent masochists religiously trek to North Wales every year? Two riders, both with 22 attendances under their Belstaffs, are Brian Watson of Wolverhampton and Brian Rees from Bridgend. Brian explained: "This was the first rally I ever did and I've been coming every year but one, on my BSA A10-It's become a habit."

The habit seems to be spreading beyond Britain's shores, with riders from Eire, Belgium, Holland and France attending this years event.

Farthest-travelled club award went to the newly formed Les Baboussets from Grenoble in France who battled through blizzard conditions on their way. Spokesman Andre Chard-onnet said; " There was a stage, when we hit snowdrifts three feet deep, that we thought we'd never make it- it's all part of the fun!"

Dragonists arrived on a selection of weird and wonderful machines from a turbo-charged Trident to a Mini-Cooper 1100 engined outfit, but this years special award went to Philip Kirk of Dudley with a Zundapp 200-powered Bantam military outfit he built in three months for a cost of just £60. He said; " I have been riding bikes for a decade and one day decided I'd end up with the bike I want, only if I Built it myself."

Other award winners were Patrick Lowe with a well used but immaculate Vincent Black Shadow, which won the best vintage prize.

Chairists award went to Tony Luker of Abingdon, while distance awards went to two foreigners, Jean Claude Taglainut of La Ravooire, France, and Dennis de Baek from Brasschaat in Belgium.

Written by Paul Myles

A WINTERS TALE 1984

Came the day of the Dragon; it was grey, cold and sleeting, and although the weather forecast looked good for north Wales we still had to get there, some 300 miles. The Jawa buzzed along quite merrily, although it could not be persuaded to exceed 50mph, apart from those occasions when we were overtaken by giant trucks on the M1, which then cut back to the inside lane rather sharply, at which the outfit would respond like a junk under full sail in the trucks slipstream, until thoughts of the rather spongy brakes would force me to ease off and break the tow. The full fairing offered good protection, although magnifying considerably the noise from the two-stroke motor. Motorway driving is tedious at the best of times.

Still we had a long way to go and we were determined to break the back of the journey in the shortest possible time-and 50mph doesn't help to achieve that. For Big Terry on the Kawasaki it must indeed have been a frustrating ride.

The gallant Kawasaki 440 LTD with Big Terry and a mountain of gear aboard. The willing little stead was also to carry the photographer-all 6ft 3in and 17 stone of him.

By mid-afternoon we were up as far as the last services before the turn-off for the A5 to Telford and we stopped to replenish both the bikes and ourselves, as well as to try and get warm, for by now we were frozen to the marrow.

A plate of fish and chips and several steaming hot mugs of tea and we were ready to face the world again. Trouble was, the Jawa wasn't. Not even after pushing the wretched thing around the car park for a half-a-dozen laps would it start. The mechanic from Boardman's Recovery, based at the services area, accepted the proffered RAC card, even though they were affiliated to the AA, and kindly checked through the wiring with his electronic testing devices. Finding nothing noticeably amiss, we again cleaned and set the points, gave it a push, and bingo! the beast fired. We loaded everything aboard again and set off up the M6.

Off at junction 12, slow down at the roundabout at the top, open up again down the A5 and- back on one cylinder. Spitting and coughing, we limped along the road in search of a garage or similar where we could either work on or leave the bike altogether, when suddenly it burst again into full song, this coinciding with the appearance of a little red light on the dash, an indication that the battery wasn't charging-and then I began to remember a phrase in Arnold Handley's write-up in the *Sunday Express*: " On the first night the generator, set wrongly at the factory, couldn't handle the power of the headlight. So the battery drained flat and everything died."

We had planned to spend the night in Shrewsbury and it became a race against time along the ill-lit busy road to reach the town before the battery lost all its charge. We lost. Suddenly the engine cut out and would only run if the lights were totally switched off. With Terry off-set behind me, lighting the way for both of us with the Kawa's splendid headlight, we cautiously travelled the remaining 10 miles into Shrewsbury.

A WINTERS TALE

This delightful little county town is well served with bed and breakfast houses and Mrs. Martin's establishment in Abbey Forgate provided warm, comfortable beds, colour TV in the bedroom and a gargantuan breakfast for only £5.50 per head. Most welcome.

Next morning, wonder of wonders, the Jawa started first kick-something it had never proved capable of since we took delivery, and this with a flat battery. Must be a reason somewhere? Loaded up, off we went again towards the north-west frontier, the bike running Quite sweetly, if somewhat underpowered as the hills became gradually steeper when, about 10 miles from Llangollen, the dreaded misfiring started again. Previous attempts at diagnosing the faults had proved fruitless, so we determined to limp on as best we could to reach our objective, meantime being overtaken by an ever-increasing stream of bikes of an extraordinary variety.

Perhaps someone can explain to me the strange compulsion that present-day riders of Brit bikes have to wear the filthiest and tattiest raiment? Almost invariably riders of Japanese or continental machines were smartly turned out in leathers or traditional Belstaffs, where-as the rag-tag-and-bobtail minority aboard old Beezas and Matchlesses with outrageous "ape hangers" (what an appropriate expression!) wore old overcoats shredded almost to streamers, jeans with huge holes in the knees, and old army boots-some without laces in them- while crash helmets had apparently had the linings removed, such was the low profile obtained. It was bitterly cold, and how they bore the elements was a complete mystery to me.

Bala in North Wales was the point at which we would follow the route to the control caravan. Unhappily it was also the point at which the Jawa was to cry 'enough', for the sparks disappeared altogether and we had to enlist co-operation of Williams garage in the main street, where we could leave the outfit under lock and key until arrangements could be made for the Jawa to retrieve it.

As I mentioned earlier, we had taken a whole load of gear with us to ensure our comfort. Big Terry is 6ft 2in and weighs 161/2 stone; I'm 6ft 3in and 17 stone. Both of us, in voluminous layers of winter riding attire, with two tents, two air mattresses, two sleeping bags, camping stove, tin mugs, plates and food for two days piled (with the aid of one dozen bungees) on to the unsuspecting little Kawasaki! We did however, leave behind a large sack of potatoes in the sidecar.

We would so easily have forgiven the kawa if it had handled like a pig, if it had lacked performance, or had inadequate brakes. It showed shortcomings in none of these areas. The route from Bala up the A4212 to Trawsfynydd to join the A470 to Ffestiniog and Blaenau Ffestiniog, over the Crimea Pass, is very mountainous and, with odd patches of ice, could have presented a few problems. However, the willing little bike soared up the hills and proved to be sure-footed, with adequate braking power, despite its most unwarranted load.

The control caravan located, we were given our tickets and the route, which lay through some breathtaking scenery to the rally site, which was to be found located just off the A5, soon after the pretty village of Betws-y-Coed.

A WINTERS TALE

THE Dragon, ran into a bad spot some years back owing to its attraction for an increasing number of yobs and yahoos whose behaviour threatened cancellation for the event, leading to its being restricted in numbers by introduction of a positive tickets-in-advance policy. This system appeared to have done the trick although unfortunately in 1982 a rival event was held close to the Dragon Rally site and the behaviour of the participants was appalling, with local pubs and village amenities being vandalized, that the local police apparently reluctant to sanction the Dragon for 1983.

The weather was relatively mild for, talking to some of the regular rallyists, they had often had to contend with huge snowdrifts and blizzard conditions in other years but, for us, it was nevertheless bitingly cold. Based in the National Trust area, with splendid views of Snowdonia, the rally attracted something like 1,500 enthusiasts, many of them from the Continent. They arrived on a weird and wonderful selection of machinery which ranged from the latest and greatest custom-made models costing a small fortune to ingenious home-made specials powered by anything from a Mini Cooper to an old Bantam engine.

But for my money the man who should have stolen the show, but whose deeds went largely unnoticed, was the chap (his name, to my chagrin, I have lost) came all the way from Penzance in Cornwall, riding non-stop for 17 hours, aboard a 1964 Honda 50 cc step-thru.

" My Bee-Emm had broken down just before I was due to leave," he explained, and I've come on almost every rally for the past 22 years, so I wasn't going to miss this one!"
A cardboard box served as his "top box" to carry his equipment and a gallon can of oil was strapped to the carrier just in case he needed it.

" But I needn't have bothered," he said. "It's run like a sewing machine the whole way and used not a single drop of oil. I've come just about the whole way on the hard shoulder of The M5". And don't anybody ever tell me that Japanese motorcycles don't last or aren't reliable!

The Abundance of driftwood in the area of the stream bank where we pitched our tent, a little away from the main concourse and hi-fi cacophony, enabled us soon to have a roaring camp fire where, after consuming a mountain of sausages and beans, we had a few heart-warming nips of the amber fluid brought "for medicinal purposes only" and got on with the serious business of rallying- the banter and the chaff, tales of misfortune and derring-do, and hilarious adventures of the rallyists en route to the event.

Big Terry just sat and looked at his Dragon rally badge as if he had been awarded the VC! " I'm going to have some more of these," he said. With a hangover, an inflatable mattress that didn't stay that way, a compulsion to make frequent water during the night and a sleeping bag designed for a midget, I didn't exactly have a five-star sleep that night, but in the morning the fire embers were still glowing and it wasn't long before they were coaxed into a blaze and coffee and more beans and sausages were on the go.

A WINTERS TALE

We had decided on making the journey home to Hertfordshire in one hop and early packed up camp and loaded everything back on the Kawa-to the incredulous stares and grins of the other rallyists.

It proved impossible for either of us to tolerate being either passenger or driver for more than 20-30 miles at a stretch. The former because of the acute discomfort on the back, particularly from the grab handle immediately behind the seat which jarred most painfully on the base of one's spine, and the latter because of the bitter cold which penetrated thick fleecy-lined gauntlets and waxed cotton overmitts to an excruciatingly painful degree. Of course it must be said that the bolt-upright position dictated that one's body took the maximum blast from the wind although the bike being so grossly overloaded with two abnormally large bodies, one can hardly blame the designer for inflicting bruises on both our backsides by means of the grab handle!

Our friend Taffy ran out of juice on the way to the 1984 Dragon. Photograph by Dave Pearson.

Anyway discomfort apart, the Kawa performed in flawless fashion, taking it's huge load without a mummer of dissent the whole 280 miles home, at the legal limit, only punctuated by breaks for fuel or in a lay-by to run, leap and flail arms around like a dervish in an effort to restore warmth and circulation.

And, would you believe, after a round trip close on 600 miles, that Gates Poly Chain toothed belt needed not the teeniest bit of re-tensioning.

And the Jawa? Well, I'm sure that it's not really such a bad motorcycle-but rather that it had not been properly prepared for the job it had to do.

All the same, it would have been appreciated if Jawa had compensated in part for a great deal of inconvenience by at least letting us know what was the problem with the electrics that had troubled both myself and the man from the *Sunday Express*. Perhaps I wouldn't have minded so much about losing my sack of potatoes!

Written by J.K.H for the Motorcycle Sport

'I think it will fit here' getting ready for camp at the 1984 Dragon at Pant-y-Cyff, Pentir near Bangor. Photograph by Dave Pearson.

DRAGON DRIFT-BUSTERS 1985

Blizzards and driving snow drifts dampened the fire of the 24th Dragon Rally weekend. Treacherous conditions kept away two-thirds of the estimated 1,800 entries, but 600 hardy souls battled their way through to reach the Gwrych Castle venue in Wales for a trip they will never forget.

News Bulletins reporting that Wales was virtually cut-off turned many bikers back, but for those who carried on, the organising Conway Club provided warm food and whisky on arrival.

George Theissen's Guzzi Nuovo Falcone meets the treacherous snowbound, Horseshoe Pass.

Out of the 600 who arrived, nearly half were solos.

George Theissen, from Luxembourg made an epic trip aboard a 500 Moto Guzzi with a broken gearbox. A railway worker with a special pass that would, give him free travel home, George said he would rather ride back despite only having two gears available.

For Rally Review Magazine reps Zeb and Vic, travelled two-up on a Norton Commando, it took more than nine hours to get there. " We only fell off once, but we didn't do much damage," said Zeb.

But for Bollards' scribe Willy, it wasn't such a smooth journey. After falling off five times, he turned back. "I reached Telford and decided to call it a day, then I fell off again on the way home."

The venue, which was one of the original Dragon sites, proved easier to reach for Stockport bikers Paul Blacklock and Ken Chaplin. The lads must have been wise to the prevailing weather and arrived aboard a 1300 cc Mini converted into a trike via a BSA A10 front end. Said the builders: " We had no problem getting through the snow drifts and negotiating the ice."

Some of the best prepared for the conditions though, were Anvil M.C.C. Club member Glyn Nash arrived, boiled some water on the stove and filled his water bottle which was rapidly passed along to Mick and Dave Grove, Jack and Craig Turley, then eventually Debbie Bosworth. As shown in the photograph.

DEATH OF A FALCON

The weather was cold and rainy (turned later to snow) when we started in Luxembourg. This year it was George Theissen on his old Moto Guzzi Nuovo Falcone and I , Jerry Frantz on my Yamaha 500 XT. It was George's fourteenth Dragon Rally and my second.

When travelling to Oostende we had no troubles, except the usual gremlins with a frozen carburettor on George's Guzzi.

Jerry Frantz continuing his journey to the Dragon from Allan Carr's.

We arrived in the afternoon at Oostende and sailed on a ferry to Dover. In Britain it was warmer than on the Continent and the weather was quite fine. A few miles away we camped for the night.

The awakening next morning was accompanied by heavy rain that didn't stop for the whole day. We rode north on the M25, around London then up the M1, we had to reach Birmingham to visit our friend Allan Carr.

This time my XT had some minor troubles due to moist electrics. That was quickly repaired and I rode on. Meanwhile George had continued on his way.

Due to heavy rain, the already dense traffic on the M1 became a very slow stop and go. A car in front of me was even slower than the rest of the queue, so I decided to pass.

Unfortunately I forgot my sidebags, and hit the car's taillight, which broke. The bag was torn off, but was easily repaired with a spare tube. To my great astonishment 6 or 7 people climbed out of the car (it was a simple saloon car). It was a whole Pakistani family. They were quite afraid and worried about their car, but when I gave them £15.00 for the repair, all was OK.

Continuing on the M6, at approx, 10 miles before Birmingham, there appeared a motorcycle parked on the hard shoulder. One person was busy around it. It was George! His Guzzi had a gearbox failure and the 3rd and 4th gear could not be used. So George decided to continue in second gear and have a try at repairing it at Allan's home. But unfortunately a gear change fork was broken or bent. So trying to get a spare part for a twenty-year-old rare Italian Lady, in Britain?.... So the Falcone had to go on to North Wales in second gear. George left early in the morning the next day (in second gear his Guzzi was really slow). I left Birmingham about two hours later in heavy snowfall.

All went well until about 10 miles past Shrewsbury. Meanwhile a thick blanket of snow covered the road. Travelling at 30 miles per hour on an A road, suddenly my engine stopped. It happened just beside a lay-by. Well, I thought, that's just right, and steered on to it. A hundredth of a second later I was sitting on my bottom in the middle of the road! the XT lying on my feet. What had happened? This lay-by must have been the only one in Britain where a kerbstone had to be ridden over to gain access.

Snowbound in Llangollen 1985

DEATH OF A FALCON

The stone was of course hidden by the snow. I waited for more or less ten minutes, contemplating the bike and its heavy load from a rather unusual angle. I was unable to move myself or the bike even for the slightest part of a inch.... A car appeared, stopped and two horrified men jumped out. I had to explain what happened and finally they lifted the XT off my feet. Apart from a little pain on my big toes, I was OK. (the nails turned black by the evening). George and I had decided to meet at the Horseshoe Pass for bivuak. Arriving there, I tried to climb the Pass, but was unsuccessful. A tyre print was clearly visible going to the top. I could not believe that George was able to climb the pass with his heavy loaded Guzzi, despite him being, if not one of the best, motorcycle riders I have ever met.

The control caravan site, ever so slightly snowbound.

Finally it began to darken and I abandoned the climb and turned back. Arriving at the entrance of Llangollen, I noticed signs of light on the road, it was George. He had also tried to climb the pass but hadn't been any more successful than me. In fact the tyre print came from a trail bike who had passed five minutes before my attempt. I put my tent up beside George's, had a meal (from can), and fell asleep.

Next morning the temperature was minus 18 and my black toenails were rather painful, so painful that I could not wear my boots, somehow, they got too narrow during the night. After several attempts, I put my slippers on and walked carefully to Llangollen, and into an outdoorshop to buy the biggest wellies they had in stock. Now well equipped, the ride could go on without problems, to the rally site at Gwrych Castle.

The rally was very enjoyable, we had a lot of fun, as usual. Sunday morning, we got up early, to ride to Dover. The temperature was still very low, (minus 20 C, rising to 15 C). For that reason I decided to follow George at his slow speed (35-40 mph) in second gear only!

The motorways were free of snow, and we advanced slowly but surely.

Camping in the grounds of Gwrych Castle in freezing conditions.

DEATH OF A FALCON

George's falcon began to make a funny noise: Boum-Boum-Boum, suddenly it happened-forty miles north from London. Boum-Boum-Boum-ccccrrangkk------silence. George stopped in the emergency lane. I stopped behind him, climbed off my XT and went over to George to look at what had happened. George was still sitting on his bike and just said: "That's it, Guzzi time over."

The next morning at Gwrych Castle.

I towed George and his Guzzi Falcone to the next exit. He then called Allan Carr to organise transport to Dover. Next morning Allan and Paul came with Allan's trailer. We put the Guzzi inside and rode to Dover. When we arrived, I towed George's Guzzi on board the ferry. At arrival in Oostende it was the same procedure. I towed George to the railway station, where he put it in the luggage office.

Normally that wouldn't of been possible, but George is a railywayman, so it was no trouble organising this.

George went home by train for free (I think, railwaymen are a bit like the Mafia!), and I carried on my faithful XT.

George's Guzzi loaded up for the journey home.

At about 15km from my home I had a rear flat tyre. The valve was torn off the tube because I lowered the pressure to get better grip in the snow, and on the motorway there had been no possibility to refill because the valve was frozen. My spare tube had already been cut into strips and used to repair my sidebag damaged in the car accident. I had to call my girlfriend, (not yet my wife) to pick me up. It was a Dragon adventure to always remember.

Written by Jerry Frantz

CONWY & DISTRICT M.C.C.

Dragon Rally 1985

Sat./Sun., 9th/10th February

ENTRY TICKET

The site of the control will be sent at the end of January.

This ticket must be produced at the control before proceeding to the camp site.

Signature ....

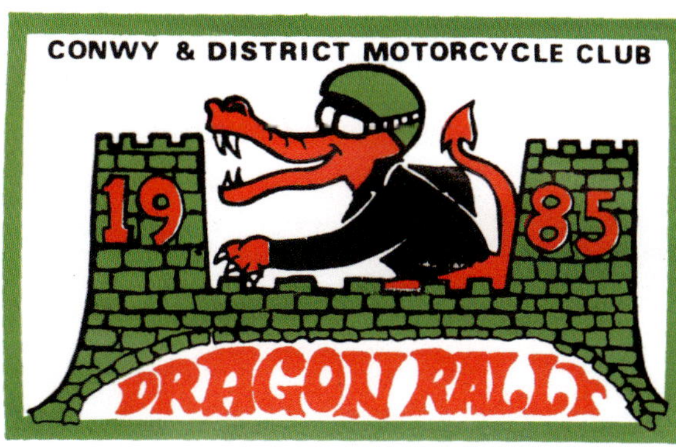

THE DRAGON THAT NEVER WAS

A small group of us decided it was time to attempt the Dragon Rally, this comprised of myself: Geoffrey Fairhead, my brother David Fairhead and Chris Hunter.

Dave and I left off work at One o'clock Friday afternoon on the 8th February and got home on the works bus to get changed and sling final things in chairs ready to leave with Chris at Two o'clock. Forecast: Snow in East Anglia changing to rain coming in from Wales, So no snow in Wales we thought; (wrong! poor fools to listen to weather men). I intended to sleep in my chair as it is nearly 8 feet long 36 inch wide, with radio and two interior lights. David, after much thought, decided to do the same, although his chair is a bit smaller. Chris, with all his sports type chair was taking his family Rolum ridge tent.

Dave and I both had heated grips and we all had handle bar muffs and full fairings, as a precaution for a cold journey ahead. I also took jump leads and a hand pump for petrol. Apart from this we all took the normal tools and jackets etc. I also took a wind break and some polythene sheet. Plenty of thermal underwear, boots, layers of clothes and Dave and I also took Gaz heaters.

It started to snow as we got ready, and indeed it had been snowing all morning. Chris arrived on time and we got on our bikes. " Which way", said Chris, (as he wanted to go by the A5 but was out voted so wasn't sure of the way). As we drove off on the road my horn started sounding (I had two Austin 1100 horns fitted and one had caused trouble the week before so I had removed it thinking that this was the trouble. I removed the other one and tied up the wires. (sort them out when we get back). So off we went again.

The next problem was snow clogging my visor so I flipped it up but it was not tight enough, after passing the town of Diss we stopped and I took it right off the helmet. I then found that although I had on an under helmet, the wind was burning my face but fortunately for me Chris wanted to stop at Bury because of a funny noise from his front wheel, (snow and ice building up) so I took the opportunity to put on a leather face mask.

Next stop St Neots, after passing one or two lorries and cars in various forms of distress on the Newmarket bypass. We had coffee and sandwiches and David took over the lead for the next stage. Just through Bedford, stopped for twenty minutes at a narrow bridge, a lorry was stuck behind a stalled car, it was still snowing on and off.

We got to junction 14 on the M1 (Newport Pagnell) around 7 or 8 o'clock, a lorry driver let us all in together off the slip road because the motorway was completely blocked with vehicles as far as the eye could see.

Chris had enough petrol to miss the first services because the next one was only 13 miles. We covered the next 10 miles in about an hour and a half.

I have never been on a road surface like it. The tracks cleared by the other vehicles were like iced cobbled stones. A few incidents come to mind during that hour and a half.

Which way now? heavy snow causes diversions to the Dragon. Photo by Bruce Pollard.

THE DRAGON THAT NEVER WAS

A despatch rider gingerly picked his way through the lines of vehicles. A few solo riders, presumably going to the Dragon Rally. A rider laying his hands on his engine. And a car driver changing a wheel (what luck).

The fumes are chocking, and we found out what the delay was, Road works two miles, SORRY FOR THE DELAY! At last I get into second gear. Thank goodness for the fan on the engine keeping it cool and me warm. We were on the hard shoulder as they were using it as a lane and the bikes began to slide from side to side on the ice and snow.

We stopped at Rothersthorpe services, Chris had a meal and Dave and I had coffee (we had brought soup with us).

Cars had parked at the cafe in all directions and a car had parked across our front. Dave's bike wouldn't turn over (the battery is an original 1976). So we pushed all the bikes back and jump started Dave's bike. We filled up with petrol, there were six pumps, four were roped off, so one pump is serving two cars at a time . There was about twenty vehicles waiting. Two solo riders started chatting to us, they were heading for the Dragon, but decided they were turning back. They asked us if they knew where the next turn off was to get back on the motorway. One big fellow with a beer gut, admited he was scared to go back out there, with it been so deadly.

But we decided to press on and got off the M6 at Junction 12 and found a spot till dawn. I took the lead, 30mph we stopped at Hilton services just before our turn off so that Chris could fill up.

We go on to the A5 as the M54 is said to be really bad. Dave leads, we come to a big roundabout (I am last) it's in a hollow and there is about a foot of snow on the road and Dave does a luvverly 90 degrees turn and gets stuck!

We stopped, but before we can help, four lads pull up behind in a van and run past us and help Dave turn around. They ask where we are heading, as they had seen us on the motorway. We carry on round the roundabout. The wind is blowing snow in white clouds off the banks and in front of us. We then decided to stop in a lay-by but they were too exposed, so we decide to go on the M54.

There was little traffic on the M54 but the surface was very rough. I started to hear a lumping sound coming from my sidecar wheel, and as I have two dampeners fitted I thought one might have come loose. I flashed my light at Chris and Dave and while I stopped to check they carried on. I couldn't find anything wrong, so I carried on and realised that I was now on a normal A road and I stopped at the next garage, which was well lit. I jacked up the sidecar wheel to make sure everything was fine. It was hard to turn because there was so much ice so I cleared this away with a knife. Dave and Chris rolled into the forecourt and I explained to them what had happened, so we all set off again. I put my lights on but they didn't come on, so I stopped again. I tried the spotlights but they were thick with ice. Chris held the torch for me and I fixed the blown fuse. We were now stuck in sub-zero temperatures with a blizzard raging around us. We set off again.

We arrived at the R.A.C box off Shrewsbury by-pass, No R.A.C. men, they have more sense! So we put the bikes around the hut and settled down for a sleep.

THE DRAGON THAT NEVER WAS

At 4 o'clock on the Saturday morning, I put on my gas heater and had the rest of my coffee and sandwiches before getting into my sleeping bag. The wind was howling, but at least it had stopped snowing. A snow plough woke me up at 5.10 am. I put the radio on, Junction 11 of the M1 was drifting with snow and some roads in Wales are blocked. Advice was do not travel unless really necessary, what happened to the rain? Dave got up at 6.00 am and woke Chris. We decided to turn back. We could get to the Rally, but would we get home!

Snow had filled my handle bar muffs, but otherwise we were OK. We start heading back. It started to snow again. Dave went in the lead onto the M54. We were in the only clear lane and this was very rough. A lorry passed us on the snow and showered us with snow and ice. Chris sticks up his fingers at the lorry driver. I found on this trip that of all the classes of driver, the lorry drivers were the most stupid. As we came across jack knifed rigs littered along the entire route. We stopped at the first services on the M6 for breakfast and to fill up.

As we passed Birmingham conditions improved for a while. But it was still so slippery that my drive wheel kept breaking traction even though I was very gentle on the throttle.

As we get on the M1 we come up behind two outfits, a full dress 1100 wing and Saluki with an across the frame four, of some sort, hitched to a G.P.Sports.

We pulled in at Newport Pagnell services for fuel and coffee. They were also heading for the Dragon but had decided to turn back home for London ,due to the bad conditions.

The roads off the motorway were bad and we were held up for 45 minutes near Bedford, so we spent the time removing ice buildup from the bikes. We then stopped along the Newmarket by-pass to fix Dave's throttle. His heated bars had loosened the grip. Chris turned off for Thetford and Dave carried on ahead of me. After by-passing Bury he appeared to have gone round the roundabout twice. There was still some very bad places where the roads were open.

I had one bad moment when the sidecar wheel dug in and swung the bike, it then let go throwing weight the other way and almost throwing me off. Luckily nothing was coming the other way. We finally got home at 4.30 pm on Saturday. Dave proceeded to get stuck in a foot of snow on his driveway.

We had been on the road for 25 and half hours and had covered 439 miles with a two hour break. My legs were stiff, my back ached and my face was sore. We may not of made it to the Dragon, but we still had an extremely eventful journey trying to get to it, and still managed to retain our sense of humour.

Was it worth it? I think so. I like driving an outfit and trying to get the best out of it.

Chris phoned on Sunday and asked if I fancied a trip to Shrewsbury? I said you could die sitting in front of the telly!

That Day nine people died in crashes between Junction 13 and 14 on the M6 and thirteen were injured. It makes you think.

Written by Geoffrey Fairhead

THE DRAGON CELEBRATES ITS 25TH ANNIVERSARY

Dragon Rally 25th sticker

Every year I wonder wether to come, but I always do, said the Ariel Owners Chairman, echoing my own sentiments. But that is moving on a bit......

As Usual the rally was a camping weekend held in February at A north Wales site, for pre-booked entrants only. But this year would be a little special, said organisers in commemoration of reaching the 25th year of the event. My usual reluctance to part with my fee a couple of months in advance was overcome because this one would be my 21st rally, and that certainly wouldn't be right to miss. Portents for the weather were not good. Snow and continuing cold in the forecasts made it sound as if there would be a re-run of last years snowdrifts. A challenge, certainly, but sometimes one feels that the difference between a challenge and being off one's rocker is rather marginal. It didn't help that a week or so earlier some near relative of the human race had stolen my riding kit (out of a padlocked security bag) from the bike in Northampton. They left me only sundry spare gear to use. (and a very cold ride home that particular night in open-toed shoes!)

At least it made the lightweight on trials tyres the obvious choice, which was just as well as it was the only bike running and taxed while the Vincent was been rebored.

A prior appointment took up the morning of February 8th, before the camping gear could be strapped on (I wasn't risking having that stolen too), and the trip up the A5 started.

There was a bit of a snowstorm around Shrewsbury, but otherwise the roads were clear, and the weather actually rather good for a ride- even sunny. It is not to everyones taste, but I find the A5 after Telford rather a nice road, even on something as slow as the Fanny B. The site was adjacent to the main road, just before Capel Curig, one that had been used before, and before the best scenery, but anyone arriving earlier could have gone for a pleasant tour around to pass the Saturday. I wasn't that early. In fact it was getting gloomy, but in spite of my thinking how few people I actually know among the rally scene now, the tent wasn't up before John West and his wife came over for a chat before leaving early. John has attended some of the very earliest Dragons.

At the signing-in there was the usual soup, and badge, but this years rallyists will be conspicuous in 1986 by their green hats featuring the Welsh Dragon. modern technology kept some entertainment going with videos; The Paris Dakar one was interesting enough to keep me a while. A hot-dog stand catering for the lazy, but otherwise there was little organised entertainment (no rock band or even a beer tent), Which kept the emphasis on a bit of socialising.

Grey Porridge as far as the eye can see, or..... workhorses still ready and willing after 30 years service; it depends on your viewpoint.

THE DRAGON CELEBRATES IT'S 25TH ANNIVERSARY

Machinery was very varied. In fact for the first time that I can remember there was a Morgan three-wheeler present (a rare sports model), and surely I don't remember a Berkeley three-wheeler before. More than the average number of British bikes turn out for the

Dragon to show that they are used somewhere, though quite where, during the rest of the year, isn't certain- there own one-make rallies, one must assume. We all know that MZs are available with a chair, but an old coach built double-adult? Heather MacGregor pointed out that the Brough Club got a number of members there, though sadly not on Broughs (more correctly, Brough Superiors....... I have yet to see a Brough in the flesh).

Perhaps the Harley- mounted American deserved exemption. He had flown over specially for the weekend! Looking round the bikes reminds one to be careful about making biased generalisations...Cafe racers with clip-ons and choppers were represented, as to was a special enclave to astound Fred O'Track: the Grey Porridge band fielded a C10, C11 and a C12 (variants of the 250 BSA, for those brought up with modern bikes). One of my friends used to be a C11 fanatic, and back in the days when I coveted things on scrap heaps C10s used to look good.

As it was a rather special year, the organisers tried to get some of the long-standing rallyists together, and they tell me this added up to over a dozen who have attended every single one. Which makes my tally look ordinary (mind you, I started as a pillion passenger to achieve that!). I didn't get details of the various award winners but I can vouch for the quality of the awards, which have always been very smart (P.U.B. has taken the " oldest Bike" a few times), and this year were very covetable- I nearly took away a beautiful slate trophy engraved with a Welsh Dragon, polished to proudly grace any mantelpiece. It would probably have broken on the way back......

CONWY & DISTRICT M.C.C.
Dragon Rally 1986
Sat./Sun., 8th/9th February
ENTRY TICKET
The site of the control will be sent at the end of January.
This ticket must be produced at the control before proceeding to the camp site.
Signature R. Morgan

It's nice to ride back along a road busy with motorcyclists, real ones with luggage and tents, off to a place 100 miles or two away.... it's one of the pleasures of making the trip, even if every one down to 50s, did go faster than my ageing heap. North Wales seemed to be the best of country to be motorcycling in that weekend...... sun again till England, then a bit of snow.

December 86 and no doubt I'll be wondering whether to go again, reluctantly sending off my entry, and then going because I'm too mean to waste the cash. Then I'll see the scenery, and meet the enthusiasts, committed motorcyclists, and return well satisfied with the weekend. Why don't you give it a try, unlikely though it sounds? Look for a bike indistinguishable from a scrap heap, and an owner who seems to covet things on scrap heaps, and have a chat.... it's probably me.

Written by P.U.B.

WAILING WALL

Terror stricken Colvin Abraham's determination to overcome his personal conflict with a wall typified the gusty, resourcefulness of 1200 riders at the 26th Dragon Rally.

The Manchester rider was one of three returning to the site on Saturday night in the chair of Tommy Hamer's Sabb-engined outfit. Fearing the law might be about to pounce, he decided to hide behind a wall until the patrol car disappeared.

Colvin Abraham re-lives the senstaion of leaping off a bridge- and to prove his love of water, slipped off the rock for another dunking!

He leaped over the wall only to fall 20 feet into a raging torrent! " I thought it was a low wall to a field," he said. "I knew there was something wrong when I vaulted over and kept on falling!"

Colvin managed to dry out at a local bed-and-breakfast house.

There was no challenge of riding wintry roads to the Capel Curig site. Instead, more riders then ever turned their annual pilgrimage into a personal battle. Scores decided to take the hard route by riding a variety of old and new small capacity bikes, including a Honda step-thru outfit, and MZ seemed to be the most popular choice.

Bitzas, customs, specials and outfits from the grotty to fine classics completed the picture of riders overcoming massive odds to earn another badge. These days you lose all 'Dragon cred' by opting for something reliable and Japanese! but they could be used as a last resort.

Dragon men are nothing if not determined. Like Dave Thomas of Luton. His Guzzi T3 seized its starter motor just before the weekend. No way was he missing his 25th Dragon, so he went to London, hired a Honda VT500 for £50.00 and made it to Wales.

Derek Morrison's trip from Birmingham was a catalogue of disasters. First a luggage strap broke on the M54, and many miles later he realised it was missing. "We went back, found my sleeping bag, but no tent. Someone else had beaten me to it!" Said the electrical engineer.

He Left his breakfast eggs scrambled on the road and carried on, only to have the 58 350 Velocette seize up just 20 miles from Llangollen!

So for the second year, he rode into the rally on the pillion of a Honda. In 1985, he had a puncture in Corwen.

All hands to the wing-it took a lot of muscle power to extract this weighty outfit from the Welsh mud.

WAILING WALL

A very ratty Jawazuki, which didn't betray owner Ian Brookes's degree in engineering, completed a hat-trick of failures when it broke down for the third time on the way home. The Coventry man's rear wheel collapsed again under the strain of lugging a lightweight chair.

There was also a story told of a rider married on Saturday and sleeping alone at the Dragon!

The site of the Dragon rally at the popular Riverside site by Capel Curig in 1987. Photo by Rod Morgan

Nostalgia ruled on Saturday evening when the first Dragon song sheet for 17 years kept a crammed marquee ringing with popular oldies-this will again become a regular feature.

Still pondering the future of the rally, the Conwy and District Club handed out questionnaires to gauge opinion on the event.

"I'm going to go through them all and work out just what people want," said Carl Davies."Any good ideas will appear at the next rally."

Dutchman Branko Pokorny, at his fifth Dragon with a party of Harley Davidson Club riders, summed up the rally well when he said: " I like the rally as it is. It's 'unorganised' which leaves it up to the riders to make their own rally," he said.

AWARDS

Furthest Distance: male- Thierry Echenard fromVvarrens, Switzerland (870 miles).

Female: Julia Simpson, Bedfont, Middlesex (242 miles).

Furthest travelled: Alan Morris, Ellon, Aberdeenshire, (606 miles).

Oldest combined age of bike and rider: Mike Edwards (49), Ilkeston, Derbyshire, riding a 1935 Brough Superior combination.

Written by Terry Snelling

THE DRAGON GETS A SOAKING

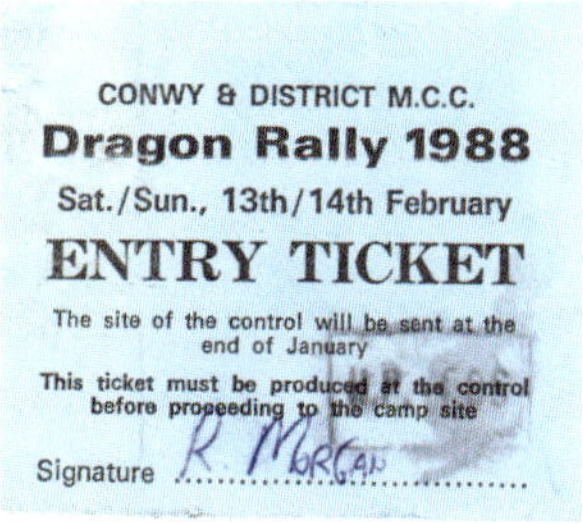
CONWY & DISTRICT M.C.C.
Dragon Rally 1988
Sat./Sun., 13th/14th February
ENTRY TICKET
The site of the control will be sent at the end of January
This ticket must be produced at the control before proceeding to the camp site
Signature ...R. Morgan...

It doesn't always rain in Wales, honest it doesn't. It wasn't raining when I took a snap of Gary's Streetfighter at Abergavenncy-not a drop. I'm off to Monmouth in half an hour and the forecast is almost good.... It did rain however, during this year's Dragon Rally.

It rained like a major distribution of the earth's ocean system. Our lads Caz and Clugg went along-and bravely brought back the damming evidence you see in the photograph.

But then Caz is an intrepid white-water canoeist anyway, so it was probably second nature to him!

Dragon Rallyists, before the Great Adventure, outside the Little Chef.

The turnout was good-around 1200 loonies rode up into the Snowdonian lofty bits, little thinking they were going to be re-enacting the style of First World War trench warfare. The CB500 from Liverpool, in the photograph below, was lucky. I took some pix of some bikes sunk up to their axles, but the rain on the camera lens made them unprintable, but then it's all good clean/dirty fun, isn't it.....?

Caz reports that a fair number of rallyists collected their greatly-prized rally badges at the gate, and then turned back- 'wimps" was the word used. I think they're all real heros-February's a month for hibernation so far as I'm concerned. Some such are the Wirral Triumph Owners, who you can see assembled at a relatively dry Little Chef before their Great Adventure. Kayak Kaz aside I reckon it's probably like winter potholing- only without the claustrophobia. Things could always be worse; honest.....

By Steve

A CB500 on site at Nant-Gwynant, Beddgelert, after the intense rain experienced at the 1988 Dragon Rally.

WHAT A WASH OUT! BUT MUD CAN'T SLAY THE DRAGON FOLK.

Not even the fingers of the 27 Dutch visitors could have plugged enough holes to stop a Dragon Rally flood!

For it was no leaking dyke that made it a waterlogged Welsh weekend- but holes in the sky where rain came in. But, like nearly 1200 other riders, that big Dutch party didn't let the deluge get in the way of a good time. They found high spirits enough to shine through the gloom. So many Dutch riders invaded the valley, a rider explained, because the Elephant Rally (usually staged about this time) had been cancelled, and they chose the Dragon to provide a winter riding adventure instead.

Early arrivals on Saturday had watched with dismay as rain lashed by a gale force wind rapidly put much of the flat, lakeside under water. It would have been an ideal venue in the sun, but its very flatness worked against the rally while the wettest weather for some 20 Dragon years was enough to force even hardened rally folk to turn back home.

An estimated 100-plus riders turned back on the road after collecting their badges. This left the rest squelching about muttering " It's a nightmare",- but the wind dropped to allow campers to cook food and for the all important bonfire to roar away and help dry wet clothing. Tents were baled out, tent poles broken by the wind were repaired, and the survivors packed a too-small marquee to swap tales. No one seemed to notice a planned 'sing-along' leader had failed to turn up.

Sunday's scene looked like the 'Somme' after a storm. While more high winds and rain battered the packing campers, Snaggletooth from Northampton's Drunken Bums MCC told me: " I've already punched myself in the head this morning! I'm the rally sec and I'm responsible for bringing people through the floods and into this. And we didn't even have a decent shelter!" No wonder so many rallyists stayed in the marquee overnight.

One of the Conwy Club organising team said there was talk of a second marquee for next year to give people a better chance of drying out.

Dragon of '88 seems destined to get into history as a real endurance test. Many riders will no doubt look back and find the best memory was of getting out of wet Wales, and onto dry roads. That's when Dragon rallying doesn't seem so bad, after all.

Slip sliding across the Dragon quagmire. Late arrivals joined the desperate search for a dry spot to camp.

THE DRAGON'S GOOSE GETS COOKED!

Semi-roast goose flambe, all set to put a new dimension on the salmonella scare, summed up the spirit of the weekends Dragon Rally, held at Capel Curig this year.

In the makeshift open-air kitchen of Fleetwood and district MCC, they showed motor cyclists can take a drama out of a crisis. Pouring rain and swamp conditions proved too much for the lesser souls, but Fleetwood folk rose to the challenge to muddle through- with the accent on mud. They were determined their annual brush with Haute Cuisine 'a la Dragon' wouldn't be jeopardized by mere bad weather. Head chef and restaurant manager were Philip Lee and Dave Barlow, or vice versa. "Hello, Philip" we say. "Whats the typical rally menu?" " were only here for the friendship and cuisine, you understand," says Philip. " So we usually have two pheasant, one duck, two trout, a panful of curry and about 12lb of steak".

Food, glorious mud. Pass the goose, get it warmed up, and get stuck in! At the 1989 Dragon Rally.

Before I could order, someone trod on the pheasant and it was lost under six inches of mud, Ah pheasant's off. Whats that thing floating over there! A glove. We can't think of a suitable sauce, apart from mud, so that's laid aside.

Potatoes were surviving well in their natural habitat, so they were kicked under the brazier. But the chef's 'piece of resistance' was the goose. Rally appetites being what they are, Fleetwoods technique was to shove a spit through it and put it on the fire, never mind the burning feathers, speed is of the essence.

No doubt Edwina Currie would have observed that most of the food handled by Fleetwood was infected by salmonella and mud.

But this only adds to the unique Dragon atmosphere."We've been doing the Dragon every year for ten years", adds Philip. " The rain was worse last year, but we picked a worse pitch this year. See you next year!"

Can't wait to see the menu.

Bomber Thomas(right) and fellow member with the Dragon Rally motif, Capel Curig.

THE DRAGON REACHES THE 1990S

The Dragon headed into the 90s with it celebrating two milestones, both its 30th and 35th anniversaries. The 30th in 1991 and the 35th in 1996. Most of the rallies were held at the popular site of Riverside near Capel Curig, with exceptions of 1994 at Garth Farm ,Twinlakes near Capel Curig and the 1996 rally at R.A.F Llandwrog near Voryd Bay by Caernarvon Airport. The later been the 35th anniversary.

The enthusiasm and the numbers began to dwindle away slightly as it was hardly covered in motorcycle magazines during this decade.

The rallyists who sent in stories say it was the 'same ole' Dragon Rally, so it had began to loose some of its charm amongst hardened all weather bikers. Also many of the motor cyclists who attended some of the early Dragon Rallies were now older, and not able to attend this rally in the middle of winter like they did in their youth, due to- quite often- wet and severe weather conditions.

There was plenty of variation in the weather patterns during this decade of the Dragon Rally, but nothing as extreme as what was experienced during the last three decades.

Conwy Club stalwarts Ken Davies, Bryn (Bomber) Thomas and Glenys Thomas are the only club members to survive all 35 Dragon Rallies.

THE DRAGON FIGHTS AGAINST A GALE!

After every Dragon (this was my sixth) I seem to get home soaked to the skin and swear blind I'll never go again. I also vow to buy a new tent that won't leak and invest in a decent set of waterproofs. Just goes to show I never keep to my resolutions.

When the 10th February arrived I was actually looking forward to the rally - probably because there is sod all else happening in February. My mate Hawk left Winchester in his cage at 4am and headed for Wirral. He's been trying to rebuild his T120 Bonnie for many a year with no joy. After a cuppa we set out for Two Mills on my T140 to meet the rest, 15 of us this year from our club on a variety of machinery; four Triumphs, two Wings, CB750, DT250, GPZ11 and a BM.

Dragon rallyists take a break at the Sportsmans Inn. Photo taken by Dave Pearson.

The Gold Wings, for all the slagging they get, do come in handy for this kind of thing. One had a chair and both were towing trailers full of heavy gear, frame tents, barbecues, even garden chairs.

The journey to the control caravan was damp but uneventful, apart from a refreshment stop at the Sportsmans Inn on Denbigh moors, claimed to be the highest pub in Wales. Hawk and I were last away after taking a few photos and the Bonnie's rear wheel stepped out once or twice as we raced down the twisty alleged A road to catch up with the pack.

Checking in at control near Betws y Coed, heavy winds blew one of the trumpets over, taking the Kwacker and CB750 down with it. Cue panic-stricken owners rushing to pick up their steeds, luckily no damage. Actually Todd, owner of the double rat award winning Honda, wasn't too concerned about another scratch or two. We pressed on to the site at Capel Curig, same as the year before.

Getting on to the site Les's Wing went down twice in the mud as he struggled to keep hold of it. At least the trailer with all the gear in stayed upright. The rest of us made it over the swamp without falling off. Combo Colin on the Wing outfit with trailer got by with a little help from his friends - at one stage there were eight people pushing the contraption!

Ever tried putting a tent up in a force ten gale? Not easy but we managed it somehow, then just as we finished a hailstorm hit the site so we ran for shelter to the frame tents. We'd slung a huge tarpaulin between them to make a living room. The garden chairs were occupied on a rota system. As soon as someone got up from one, the quickest to dive on it was the winner.

Les on his Goldwing after tackling gale force winds at the Dragon Site. Photo by Dave Pearson.

The storm subsided, the barbecue warmed up and we tucked into burgers and a cuppa.

A scout returned with the news that the Tyn y coed pub up the road was serving bikers again (last year all the pubs banned us) so an expedition was hurriedly organised.
The place was heaving and a good rock selection on the juke box added to the atmosphere. As the site was hidden away in a valley anyone walking through the village would be unaware of the fact there were 1350 bikers in the area. One party of fell-walking types were visibly shocked to find the pub choc-a-bloc with rallyists and performed a swift u-turn in disgust.

In the bar we met ex-club members Caz and Clugg from Back Street Heroes, Martin and Carol from Wallasey, as well as those people you see every year at the Dragon but never quite catch their name. In no time at all it was 11.30 and we were being thrown out.

The Dragon Rally site at Capel Curig turns into a quagmire. Photo taken by Dave Pearson.

We serenaded the villagers with drunken rally songs on the way back, then it was barbecue time again and more beer. Last year I ran out of supplies so this time I was taking no chances - I brought two 4-pint bottles of mild, four ounces of baccy and a big box of cooks matches! It all disappeared, too, which accounts for my hazy recollection of the rest of the night

I came to next morning just in time to consume a breakfast of bacon and sausage which the early risers had thoughtfully barbecued. Just as we packed up and left the site the rain started pouring down, so we stopped at the Sportsmans again to dry out. By the time we left there was two inches of snow on the ground causing lots of fun on the way back.
Four bikes, including mine, suffered throttles jamming on - exciting stuff on a snowy road with a 90 degree bend just ahead! My solution was to kill the motor, keep wringing the twistgrip back and forth till it freed off, then switch on and start again coming out of the bend. It seemed to work.

Later I found the cause was a locating peg missing from the carb which allowed the slide to twist round and jam. Some minor slides occurred but nothing too hairy.
We got home at 4 o'clock, absolutely knackered. I crashed out, Hawk drove back to Winchester and some of the others held a reunion that night in their local. We had great fun at the next club night insulting the masculinity of those who didn't go - a Dragon Rally badge bestows that right upon you. Some of the lads were even talking about tackling the Elephant Rally next year - will they never learn?

Written by Dave Pearson

THE DRAGON IN THE DRY!

I'm not normally a rally freak. I like either proper custom shows, large or small, or the manic excitement of the big events. I do a few small rallies, usually because somebody I know is putting the do on, but you don't find me sat in a muddy field every weekend. No big deal, just personal preference-lots of people don't like the big shows-and it's pretty good that we all have a choice.

Bikes arriving at the Dragon site at Capel Curig, and it's warm and dry!

But after 27 years of riding, I thought it was about time I investigated the mystique of the Dragon Rally. You might hear this crap about 'you ain't a real biker till you done the Dragon', but that's bollocks. You don't have to prove you' re a biker, you just are one. But I was curious, and I have a real thirst for new experiences. So I went for a look see.

The first thing that strikes you is how good it is to be back on the road again. I don't mean the thrash to work and back that goes on all year round. I mean the rituals of loading up the bike with all the odds and sods of life on the road, and heading off to meet kindred spirits. For me, perhaps a lot of others, this was the first big do of the year. Blow away those winter cobwebs, and recall again the essence, the real truth of what we are, what we do. After a winter of fighting everything from Euro legislation to Christmas deadlines, it really does feel good to see the sun come out as you leave Chester and start trucking through the Welsh mountains. You come across riders, either alone or in small groups, all equally laden with gear, all on real working bikes, all heading to the same destination.

As you get closer to the rally checkpoint, you see little clumps of bikes outside cafes, pubs and gas stations. To me, heading to a bike event is one of the best feelings in the world- I never get tired of the buzz, the anticipation...

And the Dragon didn't disappoint, didn't fall short, didn't fail to fulfil those expectations. Maybe I'd deluded myself about rallies all those years (maybe I was just getting old....). But maybe the Dragon is special. Perhaps it's the sense of history, the element of tradition, built up over thirty years, or perhaps it is just because it's the first big do of the year. But there is a buzz to the place. Not the frenzy of something like the Bulldog, more the happening but laid back of the Magna Carta. I was getting off on the Dragon.

It was the numbers and diversities of the bikes that really got to me. A few chops and customs of course. But also road going Vincent's weighed down with camping gear.

The sidecar is a necessity at the Dragon, not just for putting your gear in, but for using as a table to make your first brew.

THE DRAGON IN THE DRY!

Old side-valve Nortons that had been on the road all their lives-not restored, just used. Brit bikes and dirt bikes, with bearded, wild eyed riders looking like they'd just come down from the hills. Every configuration of sidecar combination known to mankind, more Cossacks than you've seen in one place before, and the worlds entire collection of MZs.

An excellent example of a rat bike!

You get the marque owners gathering in discussion groups; the merits of leading link forks, the various ways to make Urals stay together, or the MZ freaks talking about dropping rope down the cylinder head (I had to stop and listen in to that one. Apparently you take out the spark plug, feed some rope down into the cylinder, and then you turn the engine over until it squashes the rope, locking it up so you can undo the crank nut. You'll need to get the rope out afterwards, so it probably helps if you don't let all of it fall down into the cylinder....) And you get the tales of previous Dragons from the old timers. 'I remember 69, the snow was so deep', holding hands out at waist level, or 'it's not like it was when we had snow every year'. And it wasn't, Saturday afternoon was mild and sunny, making for a few happy hours spent wandering round the picturesque camp site, with waterfalls and wooded riverbanks, checking out endless odd-ball bikes, and nattering to people, some you've known before, others for the first time.

Come nightfall, as the Dragons breath draws in, you remember that it's still winter. The fog is so thick most people get lost, wandering in a drunken haze asking what direction they were facing and did anyone know where their tent was? I sat with the Jolly Roger crew from Preston, drinking, smoking and playing pirates, listening to sounds from the good ship scallywag (an XS combo) while Boo impressed us with his finely tuned Tilley lamp. The tales got taller as the night got older, and the ice got thicker on every exposed surface. By the small hours it was time for a last hotdog and bed, grab a couple of hours kip before the git in the next tent started snoring, like an elephant farting an inch from your ear every 3.5 seconds, and then as dawn breaks everyone seems to fire up their bikes at once....

With a helpful sign at the gate telling us of radar traps for the next six miles, and no documents for the bike, I turned left instead and took the long way home, adding about sixty miles to the trip but getting to ride through the spectacular scenery in the early Sunday sun.

It was still bright sunshine as I followed the A55 coast road, thinking about what it must be like when it really snows. A few miles before Chester, the fog rolled back in, along with a fierce crosswind. The temperature went down as quickly as the wind-chill factor went up, and within 10 minutes that old familiar numbness fought it's way through your gloves and attacked your fingers. 20 miles later and your stomach hurts cos you feel sick because your hands are so cold. It may not of been'69, but the Dragon hasn't lost all it's teeth.....

Written by Odgie- AWoL

A SELCTION OF 1990,S DRAGON RALLY TICKETS AND STICKERS

CONWY & DISTRICT M.C.C.
Dragon Rally 1994
Sat./Sun., 12th/13th February
ENTRY TICKET

CONWY & DISTRICT M.C.C.
Dragon Rally 1995
Sat./Sun., 11th/12th February
ENTRY TICKET

CONWY & DISTRICT M.C.C.
Dragon Rally 1996
Sat./Sun., 10th/11th February
ENTRY TICKET

CONWY M.C.C.
Dragon Rally 1997
Sat./Sun., 8th/9th February
ENTRANCE TICKET

CONWY M.C.C.
Dragon Rally 1998
Sat./Sun., 14th/15th February
ENTRANCE TICKET

CONWY M.C.C.
Dragon Rally 1999
Sat./Sun., 13th/14th February
ENTRANCE TICKET

THE SUN SHINES ON THE DRAGON 1994

February the 12th-first run of the year and New Toy time. I'd reluctantly sold a couple of bikes off over the winter (I hate having to sell bikes almost as much as I love buying new ones....) but with that plus a chunk of scrimping and saving I'd invested in a Black Wing II, a big shiny Cadillac of a bike, all fairings and boxes and loud stereos-a proper piss-take. Junking the secondary fork springs and replacing them with inches of gas pipe, and adding a new set of Avon's very excellent High Load Touring tyres transformed an obscenely gross motorcycle that handled like a tit on a tray into an obscenely gross motorcycle that handled like a tit in a sleeper bra (somewhat firmer but not entirely under control..)

This Norton has lived life to the full!

No worries, I painted the sidewalls of the tyres white so it looked like a two-wheeled pimpmobile, filled one pannier with enough booze to keep a Preston Girl happy, the other with enough grub and booze to keep me happy, filled the top box with the tent and gubbins, the pillion with young NicPic, pumped up the rear shocks, cranked up the trance tunes and headed Welshwards into the mountains......

I really like the Dragon Rally. After the winter break there's nothing better than getting that first run under your belt. Before we'd even done ten miles on the motorway we were passing other bikes loaded up with the essential weekend survival kits, and all the buzz of being on a run returns, reminding you of those old familiar feelings, that the essence of what we are and what we do is to live life on the road in the company of bloody good people. After hacking your way to work and back through the ice and snow, and endlessly trying to keep the salt at bay from your alloy and paintwork, you remember that spring is coming. Another full season of runs and parties, bikes and people, sunshine and warm weather (well, warmer than December anyway...) No matter how many seasons go by-I'm clocking up 25 now, and there's plenty been riding longer than me-you never fail to get excited by the prospect of another year, another summer. Lose that buzz and you're existing rather than living, and if there's one thing that we do as bikers, it's live life to the fullest.

The Dragon was it's usual collection of bizarre bikes, trikes, combos and oddities. On a new site this year outside Capel Curig, the traditional Saturday afternoon stroll around the site provided plenty of entertainment, meeting up with people you haven't seen since last year's Dragon, and checking out Reliant-powered Ural outfits,Tritons with foot-muffs made from old oil bottles, well used road going Vincents (I counted at least three).

The Soup ladies of the Dragon, Pauline Evans, Sian Davies and Glenys Thomas.

THE SUN SHINES ON THE DRAGON

There was also old side-valve Brits hitched to humongous chairs, beaten up superdreams and still the largest collection of MZ's and Cossacks. Not that many chops, but you'll see plenty of those later in the year. Dragon bikes provide a different sort of spectacle.

Wandering down to the beer tent gets you your free badge, free Mars, Snickers and bottle of Whisky, and free soup and roll. You proudly pin the badge on your jacket, and much trading then takes place as someone tries to corner the market in Mars bars and you swap your Whisky for something a little more mellow.

Arriving on site with all the essential gear. Photo by Rod Morgan.

By nightfall you've settled round the campfire, or staggered down to the bonfire. There's no bands to watch, no lights or lasers. You just get yourself comfortable, keep drinking so your beer doesn't freeze, and devolve into the usual gentle rambling conversations about stars and satellites, motorcycles and heroic exploits, jokes, stunts, men,women, life, the universe and bullshit, before somebody empties a burning brazier of charcoal on your head (you bastards!- even if it was by accident!), and since you can't stand up properly any more you trip over your own guy ropes, destroy one of your tent poles, wrestle with your boots for about an hour and fall into bed. Smart.

Sunday morning you wake up in swirlyland, and grab another beer to clear your head (which doesn't entirely work the way you hoped it might), before shaking the ice off the inside of the tent, loading up and setting off for home.

Relaxed and happy, your head drifts off into its own thoughts as the miles roll by. Another Dragon done, another season started, another year to look forward to. Can't beat it.

Written by Odgie for AWoL

Looking over a sunny Dragon site at Garth Farm, Twin Lakes near Capel Curig.

THE DRAGON DRAWS YOU BACK

I returned to the famous Dragon Rally in 1998. I was well into my forties and was accompanied by my twenty something Nephew. Big mistake. People in their forties on barn door tourers shouldn't travel with youngsters on sport bikes. My Nephew had a GPZ900R and a young man's thirst for speed and life. I had a GTR1000 and a penchant for cruising in comfort. Not going to happen on this trip.

We left our homes in Ireland at 5am on the Friday morning and trashed the traffic for the 100 mile trip to ferry at Dublin Port. I never thought a big tourer could be so fast but when you're trying to keep up with a young man who still thinks he's immortal, you push harder. Only lost sight of him on a few occasions.

At the control caravan in Pentrefoelas.

Checked onto the ferry and, bikes secured, we headed for the restaurant. After breakfast we decided to have a little beer. The only non-Irish beer on board was pint bottles of Newcastle Brown Ale so we had a few just to create a holiday atmosphere.

Off the ferry and into Wales at Fishguard. Owain Glandwyr welcomed us with sunshine and smooth roads. Through the Welsh countryside at a pleasant pace for the first few miles then it all went wrong when we were overtaken by a Gixxer. Red mist. Gears kicked, throttles flicked, bars gripped. Young men gone.

I did keep up the pace for awhile but the monkey of self preservation that comes with age hopped onto my shoulder and I let them go.

An hour or so later after a wonderful spin through the beautiful Welsh coastline and countryside I saw the nephew and Gixxer boy in a lay-by chattin' and smoking. What happened? they snidely enquired, did you get a puncture or something? We'll meet at Betws-y-Coed next at Dil's Diner. Think you can find that ok?. Now listen here I replied, I was at the Dragon before you lot were even born so no more of that crap. Blah, Blah, Blah they chorused. What could I say, Youth. On we went and finally arrived at the campsite.

It was a beautiful site at the Waterworks in Capel Curig. Bike unloaded, picked our spot, tents erected by 2 pm. Now what? Off for a stroll to the hotel which was about a quarter mile away, and popped in for a beer.

The choice of beers was a little more than we were used to at home so we decided to start with a pint from the first tap. It wasn't that great, so we tried another. I hadn't had such freedom on a Friday afternoon for a long time. We got lost in the atmosphere as the hotel started to fill with bikers and motorcyclists. All life was there which makes the Dragon such an attraction.

THE beer and whisky flowed like streams in heaven. The hotel was now packed, drink and jokes flying back and forth, rally badges jangling on tattered waistcoats, Scandinavians in strange spiky hats, French in berets and neat beards, Germans singing beer songs and clashing glasses in time to the song, loud as could be, polite reserved English trying to keep in time but not really getting the rhythm. Welshmen singing choir songs with all their breath but for once being drowned out by the tidal wave of disparates that is the Dragon Rally.

Saturday morning we awoke in our tents, no-one could remember how. My head was pounding, heart racing from too much alcohol, I was going to die in a tent in Wales.

Someone started chopping firewood with a small axe; that person is unaware how close to being murdered and cut to pieces he was. Eventually we started to get things together just as a storm blew in on the Saturday afternoon. My tent at the time wasn't really up to the job, ok on a balmy summer's night but not in the Welsh mountains in midwinter.

A tent pole snapped with a loud crack under pressure from the wind. That's it for me, I thought, I'm off to Betws-y-Coed for B&B. Nephew said hang on for me. Tents were flung onto the bikes and we found a beautiful guest house. I cannot remember a bed that looked so welcoming. I told the nephew I was going for a nap and I would meet him later.

I never did meet him that night. I awoke at 4am to the sound of my nephew going to bed. I had slept the whole time and missed the Saturday night. At least I was totally fit for the journey home.

The next October we sent our prepaid envelopes once more, and this time I was going on my own, properly equipped for "camping out in all weathers".

Written by Tom Foley

CONWY M.C.C.

Dragon Rally 1998

Sat./Sun., 14th/15th February

ENTRANCE TICKET

THE DRAGON FLIES INTO THE MILLENNIUM

The Dragon Rally entered the millennium with renewed vigour, and different sites. The millennium site was at the old familiar, Riverside site near Capel Curig. This site was then used for the last time in 2004. The Rally was held a couple of times at Caernarfon Airport, before heading over to the Isle of Anglesey. Then in 2008 it was sited at Cae Du near Beddgelert, and it was unseasonably warm! So much so that some of the German rallyists stripped off and went for a dip in the river! Last year it was held at Glyn Bach near Rowen, which was a great site.

Sadly during this decade Bryn 'Bomber ' Thomas passed away in 2008, a dedicated member of the Conwy Motor Cycle Club, and one of the long time organisers of the Dragon Rally. Also Johnny Emms, a well know character, and avid enthusiast of the Dragon Rally, passed away in 2009.

The Dragon Rally has once again become a popular event in the Rallyists calender. With its colourful history and extraordinary tales from motorcyclists, both from this country and Europe, of battling against all the winter elements to get to the Rally.

The Dragon Rally reaches its 50th anniversary in 2011 and deserves recognition of been one of the best and longest running rallies held in this country. We all hope that it will carry on in its same familiar style for many years to come.

The Millennium Badge

The Sunday morning clear-up squad 2010 from the Conwy M.C.C, from left to right- John Willis, Ken Davies, Arfon Jones, David Jones and Dafydd Glyn Roberts.

Peter and Margaret Davies pictured at the 2010 rally, have been to most of the rallies over the years. They still own the bike they first came on, a Triumph 650cc T6.

Signing in at the caravan 2010 is Mr. Brian Watson from Willenhall. He has attended all forty-nine rallies and hopes to make it to the fiftieth.

Photos by John Willis

Y2K DRAGON RALLY (Millennium bug!)

DRAGON RALLY

20 00

CONWY CLUB

We set off for the ferry to Wales once more. The call of the millennium Dragon proved too strong for us . We had to go. We had often been to the Dragon before. Mostly we had been rained on, snowed on, blown on. Tents had been flooded, washed away in a sea of mud, covered with snow and frost and occasionally uprooted and carried off to places unknown. I can picture some straight (i.e. non motorcyclist) coming out the front door on a Sunday morning and been suddenly enveloped in a sodden smelly tent that descends from on high.

My Nephew and I teamed up once more but this time we had persuaded some innocents that this was The One; the only bike event that every real biker had to go to. Not for the summer flowering types. We gathered together the most contrasting and contrary crowd of revellers that we could find. Individually all fine but together dynamite, ready for anything.

An early 'Wing and a chair that also had a trailer in tow carrying enough gear and beer to open a small hotel. The whole outfit skimmed the roads under the load. An old BSA M 20 held together by duct tape and curses, two or three UJMs, an iron sportster that usually vibrated the rider so much he often had to be helped off the thing he would be so numb. Triumph Tiger (Hinckley) and an elderly BMW completed the orchestra.

We poured off the ferry at Fishguard into pouring rain. We set off for Betws-y-Coed on Friday noon. Four hours of constant heavy rain later, we stopped at a village pub to try and get some relief and dry out a little bit. The light was fading fast and some lads said they had never seen such rain. All were soaked through, even the most expensive of so called waterproof gear, that had never leaked before, were sieve-like under the downpour. "Waterproof means it lets the water in and keeps it in" said a lad from the west coast of Ireland that was constantly hammered by the wild Atlantic ocean," I've never seen anything like this".

At this rate we weren't going to make the rally site on the Friday so we found accommodation eventually and dried as much gear as we could.

We continued our journey on the Saturday morning in bright crisp sunshine. Completely different country to the day before. Through stone housed neat villages, scenic passes over the mountains and through disused slate quarries and into Betws-y-Coed at last. All arrived safely and still on their own machinery. More bad weather was forecast for the Saturday night and some of our crew were worried about camping out in the Welsh mountains in winter. Hints and allegations were made about hotels and guesthouses of which there were many in that beautiful Welsh town.

All were left to make their own decisions but I said all should check in at the caravan and go see the campsite first. My nephew and I had been here before and knew the campsite at the "Waterworks" in Capel Curig would impress.

Y2K DRAGON RALLY

After mugs of scalding tea and coffee at the nearby Bryn-Glo café where we were welcomed by Mrs. Cousins, decisions were made. Some decided camping in a possible storm wasn't for them and headed back to town.Tents erected, and soup, roll, and goody bags collected from the marquee, we strolled around the campsite. All sorts of contraptions - trikes, motorcycles, tents of every colour size and format. Club flags and banners hung here and there, each vying for the most outlandish, attention grabbing, humorous, or, depending on your viewpoint, stupid name. The cruiser crowd wearing leather waistcoats over jackets. Wallets on chains, beards and shaved balding heads, the streetfighter mob in their camouflage jackets and army surplus, looking a little like those sixties Mods.

Two elderly gents on ancient vintage bikes pulled in to the site, complete with billy cans and saucepans dangling and clanging. Old Panthers puffed and chuffed along, hauling rickety overloaded sidecars. Black, dark Velocettes throbbed venomously. A horribly green coloured old Indian Chief, its rider bobbing on the sprung seat post saddle as if it was a horse in canter came down the path, followed by a modern gleaming Harley Davidson.

The campsite was alive. Barbecues were starting, stoves were being lit here and there. A crowd in one corner had brought enough firewood for week. Dunno how they did it. All were in great spirits. The huge bonfire that had been constructed by the Conwy Club which had organised the event every year since 1961 or was it 1960? This was now being lit, its centrepiece was a tall tree, which, when it eventually fell over hours later, skinned my elbow on its way to ground. Near one that, if it had hit me on the head I wouldn't be writing this today (no sniggering at the back, that boy). The marquee was a tightly packed shoal of leather and textile, the occasional waxed cotton Trialmaster floated by, ladies in long coats and fingerless gloves, piercing and tattoos here and there. All life forms were here. This is the Dragon Rally.

Things changed later that night. The wind and rain came back. A couple of first timers in our company had their tent flooded and nearly died of the cold. We bunked them into our tents that were still perfect. We had been before and were well prepared this trip. We ate hot tinned beans at 2am. At some point the nephew fell into my tent overcome by the atmosphere and a little too much alcohol.

Sunday morning we dragged ourselves to the welcoming Bryn-Glo café for an enormous breakfast, so big in fact that one of our party - who shall remain nameless - who had copious quantities of beer the previous night, went outside, upchucked, came in and finished breakfast. Ah! Youth, nothing like it. This was the last, in my opinion, of the "machinery" Dragons, if you know what I mean. After the millennium the bikes and gear became more modern, as the older crowd retired, passed away, got rickets or whatever. The event still has possibly the best atmosphere of any of the great winter rallies and I can't wait for the next one. Every year is different and will put its own unique stamp on you. But you must camp. Large numbers of bikers stay in hotels and guesthouses on the same weekend and say they were at the Dragon Rally. What a waste. This is a story of my millennium Dragon Rally. It wasn't written immediately after the event so all the details may not be exactly as it was but it's how I remember it, and all stories of the great Dragon Rally are written by the heart and not the head. Long may it continue.

Written by Tom Foley

ENTER THE DRAGON

In an attempt to blow away the winter cobwebs, I'd suggested to a few friends that we have one last run out over the Christmas holidays before returning to work in the New year. The replies were a mixture of: " Taking the wife shopping"; " The bike's laid up for the winter":" Too busy"; "Taking the kids out " and so on. The real problem was that it was too cold and they didn't like to admit it!

A visit on site from the local police force, no doubt dishing out plenty of advice.

Determining to go on the icy ride alone reminded me of my first Dragon Rally back in 1965. It was held a Llyn Padarn, near Llanberis, and the weather was cold and wintry. I set out from my home in Warrington on my trusty Matchless G3 on the Saturday afternoon, but after only 25 miles my back tyre punctured and I had to pull in at Flint to make repairs. Off came the wheel and out came my Romac puncture outfit. The repair was made, and using just a primitive hand pump I put in enough air to get me to the garage.

Just as I was about to set off again, I heard the distinctive sound of a 350cc Panther on a raucous open megaphone in the distance. Seconds later an outfit thumped its way past me, also Dragon -bound. The rider was my brother Pete, who'd set out an hour later with his mate Colin Wilkinson in the chair; and was racing to catch me up. He didn't see me parked on the spare ground and sped by, oblivious to my plight. I caught up with him about an hour later.

The drama didn't end there, however, for while climbing the hills towards Llanberis, my bike cut out and I was stranded again. I removed the headlamp shell to look for loose wires, cursing because I'd forgotten to bring my torch, and I was in the middle of shouting: "I can't see a bloody thing!" when the wiring loom burst into flames!

Always a help in such times of crisis, Pete said: " There have you got enough light now?" After another temporary repair I got her fired up again, and we made our way to the campsite, where I spent the weekend shivering and moaning, and I vowed never to go camping in winter again.

I was just 17 then and never dreamed 38 years later I'd be considering a repeat performance. I just happened to be entering the 2003 biking events into my diary when I noticed that the Dragon Rally was to be held over the weekend of 8/9 February.

This Dragon's been taken for a ride.

It was a challenge I couldn't refuse, and I sent off for my £15 ticket.

By the time February came round I'd convinced Peter that it might be a good idea, and easily led, he also applied for a ticket!

THIS time we left Warrington together on the Saturday afternoon after Pete had made the journey to my home from Horncastle on his 1996 Triumph Thunderbird. For the sake of nostalgia, we opted for the old coast road route through Queensferry, Connah's Quay and Flint. Pete stayed behind my Honda CX500 outfit, Bull Terrier 'Jack' snuggled comfortably in the Watsonian Palma. This time there were no punctures - just a hair-raising incident when a huge Buzzard, clutching branches for nest building, took off at shoulder level and had to apply full throttle to climb out of a collision course with my helmet!

Alan Moston gives Pete Kelly a wake up call among a sea of sodden tents on Sunday 9th February.

Only after panicking and dropping the branch on my head did it make the diversion and fly off to safety of the nearby woods.

After a stop for coffee and hot-pot at the Beach Cafe in Abergele, we arrived at the rally control point near Pentir to collect our entrance tickets and directions to the camp site at Caernarfon Airport. By now it was cold and grey and had started to rain - by the time we arrived at the site we were soaked. As we entered the camping ground I was amazed to see a few bikes leaving with camping gear still tied to their carriers! perhaps they'd only gone along for their badge and scarf!

Leaving 'jack' kipping in the chair, we set about unpacking and erecting our tents. It was a race against time as it was almost dark, blowing a gale and the rain was getting heavier by the minute. It took about an hour before the tents were up and our meagre belongings were safely stowed inside. In this task, we were helped by our mate Alan Moston, an expert camper who had erected his own tent in only a few minutes.

This year's rally, the 42nd to be organised by the ever-friendly Conwy Club, was attended by 1,250 bikers from all over the UK along with some hardy foreign friends who'd ridden from Holland, Poland and other far-away places.

We were each given a badge, scarf, slate commemorative plaque, soup and roll, chocolate and a miniature bottle of scotch, all very well received. This years attendance compares with a regular 1,800 in the 1960s. The highest attendance was for the 1967 Dragon Rally, held at Llanberis, where 6,700 riders packed on to the site at Llyn Padarn.

Later, while huddling from the cold in the marquee and waiting for the band to strike up, we found ourselves talking to Tony Luker from Abingdon who, along with seven others, has attended every single Dragon Rally, since the first one at Bryn Bras Castle in 1962. That year Tony rode there on his Royal Enfield Super Meteor fitted with a Canterbury double-adult 'chair'. This time he made the journey on his 1988 BMW K100RT fitted with Wasp single-seat sidecar.

The dogs aboard, and the writer prepares to stuff everything but the kitchen sink into his Honda CX500.

TONY can relate many stories about his Dragon journeys over the years, such as the time he left Abingdon on his Norton 99 outfit only to find that by Worcester it had gone on to one cylinder. Having failed to sort out the problem, he reluctantly returned home. His wife, however, wasn't going to let him miss the Dragon for the first time, and suggested he try and borrow a bike. He ended up with a friend's Trition- a bit different to a 99 outfit!- and made it after all. However, it was the year of petrol rationing, and Tony hadn't accounted for the Triton's tiny one- and-a-half gallon tank

Inevitably, just north of Worcester and in icy conditions, he ran out! At first he couldn't get off the bike because he was 'frozen in position, because of the arctic weather, the clip-ons and the unfamiliar bent-over position. However he eventually managed it, and after walking two miles for petrol soon thawed out. He also had a kick-start lever shear off, but was lucky to see one for sale at the rally auto-jumble.

Brr! Tony Luker from Abingdon is one of a select handful of Dragonists who have attended every single Rally since 1962. In that year he rode there on his Royal Enfield Super Meteor-Canterbury sidecar. Seen here after filling up in the snow.

The main changes over the years have been machine reliability. It's hard to believe nowadays that Dragonists used to see roadside breakdown points organised by the various bike clubs. Mobile phones play their part in the modern world, and Tony said that from a camping point of view, the tents are 100 times better, with lightweight flexible glass-fibre tent poles and built-in ground sheets.

It was sad to see no bonfire at this year's rally- apparently there was a safety issue concerning the airfield site- but this made it all the stranger to see fireworks going off later on!

Another feature I remembered about the early Dragons was the headlamp parade, which also is no more.

We all thoroughly enjoyed the unique friendly atmosphere of the Dragon, where motorcyclists of all backgrounds enjoy a common theme.

When we arrived I could hear dozens of soaking bikers, saying: "What the **** are we doing here?" and "Never again!" But by the time we were all packing up next morning the rain had stopped, the moans and groans of the day before had changed to: " See you next year!" and " Roll on 2004." It seemed a shame not to be staying another night.

I for one, along with 'Jack' and whoever wants to join me, will definitely be back for more!

Still smiling after a damp night under canvas, this Dutch Dragonist prepares for the long ride home on his classic BMW outfit.

Photographs and write up by Geoff Kelly CBG

42$^{nd.}$ DRAGON RALLY

Sat./Sun. 8$^{th.}$/9$^{th.}$ February 2003

Welcome to the 42$^{nd.}$ Dragon Rally.

Here are the final details to the **CONTROL**. Remember you must visit the control to exchange your **PAYMENT RECEIPT** for you **ENTRY TICKET.**

THE CONTROL CARAVAN WILL BE SITED IN THE GORS BACH INN CAR PARK ON THE RIGHT HAND SIDE OF THE B4366 ROAD ABOUT ¾ MILE WEST OF THE B4547 ROUNDABOUT BETWEEN THE VILLAGES OF PENTIR AND BETHEL.

All major roads lead to the B4366 whether you arrive by the A5 from Betws-y-Coed, the A55 (west) from the North Wales coast or the new A55 (east) from Holyhead. The only exception to this being the A487 from Porthmadog when you will join the B4366 at Caernarfon. (from this road the Control will be on the left hand side between Bethel and the roundabout).

To all we want to see you at the Rally so ride safely. There is always a police presence on Rally day and they are not as tolerant as they used to be. There have been a number of really serious accidents to bikers who do not know the roads in the area which has had an impact on their activity. So you have been warned.

Now to the site this year. Excellent hard standing and level camping. **Bikes must be parked on the hard standing where directed and not on the grass. Also no fires large or small can be permitted.** Again there will not be a bonfire this year. A small price to pay for the superb site.

The site owner will have food and beer available on site. The food may be more ambitious than just hot dogs and burgers so I am told.

There is a nearby Aircraft Museum within walking distance which is well worth a visit.

There will be the same group in the marquee on the Saturday night. There will be a number of awards as usual. Forms to be handed into the marquee before 7 p.m. on the Saturday night.

Remember the Rally is for those who come on a bike and no other forms of transport will be allowed on site. Also our site is only available on the Saturday and Sunday. A lot come over on the Friday and make a long weekend of it by staying locally. The control is not all that far from the Betws or Caernarfon areas so for those that stay overnight there it should not be a problem.

Remember your SAE for next year! (leave in marquee) or email me at roland@graybrad.fsnet.co.uk in October for details.

Safe riding and enjoy the Rally.

WE WERE WET! 2004

I really should know better at my age. The Norton was laden with panniers, tote and tank bags, carrying air mattress, sleeping bag, camera, notebook and spare clothing. There wasn't room for the kitchen sink, probably because of the precious bottle of Cote du Rhone treble-wrapped in one pannier. We were riding to North Wales in February, shortly after the floods, helicopter rescues and road closures.

It might be wet and muddy but it's the Dragon!

That bottle of wine is not normal recovery gear for a trip- the Norton single end up ahead was to blame for that. It was Bruce Pollard's well worn 1951 Big 4 side valve, it's exhaust thudding and occasionally popping under load as it towed his well laden trailer through the Welsh Marches and on into the Principality. He had his tent, plus camping stove and a large pot of beef stew for his mates, and a man can't accept such weekend hospitality as that with something as derisory as a can of larger. So Cote du Rhone it was. All for my first Dragon Rally and to add a little spice, the weather men and women on the haunted fishtank had special maniacal grins as they told of heavy rain around our destination. Apparently they had as much rain in a week as East Anglia normally has in a year. Never has Norwich seemed so attractive.

Breakfast in the transport cafe at Chirk, where a bacon sarnie tasted as it only can after 50 chilly miles on a bike, then on to Betws-y-Coed and an overnight B & B before the Saturday at the rally proper.

Mr Pollard being a veteran of this event, we rode up to check the state of the site, where Conwy members greeted us with the news that there'd been several feet of water over the field a few days ago, flattening the bracken and leaving the place pretty desolate. It had also washed out a large section of the road across the site and blokes in waterproofs were labouring away, wheel barrowing in rocks and gravel to make the road passable by bike. The trucks due to bring extra toilets and the equipment for the band had been advised not to try. Oh joy.

Friday night has faded from memory, after taking a meal and getting together with a crowd so packed it had the pub walls close to bulging. I was introduced to Boo, up from Hayle 350 miles away in Cornwall, on an Armstrong MT500. He left his Commando and 1981 Harley at home: " I looked at my bikes and this one was the greatest challenge, " he explained.

A very wet and wild, Capel Curig Dragon site, that a few days before was under flood water.

IN 2003 he took home the long distance award on the same bike, then two weeks later took the same trophy at the Alternative Elephant in Germany. Boo had scrimped, saved and put himself into debt to buy his Harley new and clearly has a deep affection for the thing: " Every time I ride it I know why I like it." You can't argue with 22 years together and still in harmony, and a recent experience of a plastic rocket jokey touching his knee on the tarmac as his bike and the Harley swept round the same bend at identical moderate speeds did nothing to convince him he should change.

The Road is washed away by floods. Ever get that feeling that you might not get off the site!

We drank some strange Welsh substance, brown in colour and served in large glasses. It has an amazing effect upon those who sip it, and they find themselves talking more and more sense until they loose consciousness. Amazing stuff.

Saturday morning started early, bike blipping under the window at something like 6.00am. After a huge breakfast-well, it was to this bowl of fruit and one black coffee wimp-the party loaded up and rode back down the A5 to the initial check, where we exchanged entry receipts for passes onto the sacred site. Riding back into Betws, the sun was up and a huge rainbow spanning the valley, but this was Wales..... so just as I decided to stop and get the camera out, down came the rain.

Onto the soggy site and a warm greeting, exchanging my pass for the usual goodies-that didn't last long. Park on the remains of the road and look around for a place to pitch the tent; Bruce opted for a streamside location and rode the Big 4 in solo, then we pushed the trailer to it's weekend parking spot. With the wind getting up, pitching a large tent was a test for patience, not to mention good training for taking a three-masted brig around the Cape.

Captain Pollard arranged to lash one end down to the big Ford-powered trike of Fester from Stourbridge, and the other to his Norton. I could see the Big 4 taking off in the breeze but not that impressive three-wheeler. The rest of the night's shelter we tried to pin down with conventional pegs; I think the longest one stayed in the ground was about two minutes.

Looking at bikes struggling through the rutted mire of the streamside track, I decided to leave the Norton safely on terra-almost-firma and carry the panniers over to our pitch. My, what fun it was struggling through the mud. I'd borrowed a pair of knee length fire-fighter boots and the muck had splashed over the top.

More joy.

Getting on and off site was not an easy task with the site turning into a mudbath.

I COUNTED four Sunbeam S8 twins on site including Jim Reader's combination. We exchanged enthusiasm for this underrated bike, given long life by the amazing spares service from Stewart Engineering in rural Warwickshire. I hadn't heard that they commissioned replacement distributors because the Lucas originals weren't available, only to have orders from the Prince of Darkness to stop it. One assumes they were concerned about litigation in the event of component failure.

Chris Hawley, UK importer of the excellent Baglux tank bags and long time member of the Conwy Club, was there. The man is clearly no fool, riding in on his scooter and going back home to sleep in a warm bed; after time spent helping to clear the site, he'd earned it.

I had one of his tank bags on a succession of bikes for 12 years and only replaced it last year. Blatant plug? Don't care-it's good stuff.

Back at the permanently waving tent, beef stew was taken in good evening company as Bruce enthused over the highlights of our journey north: " A good day. I overtook two tractors!" In truth he makes good, smooth progress on an unlikely bike, long experience showing in the way he looks well ahead and backs off to avoid dramas. The essential discipline of old bike riding well executed.

Then we were off to another pub, to imbibe a thick layer of resistance to common sense, in case that instinct convinced us it was not perfectly normal to kip down in this hostile climate while gale force winds tried to move the tent into a nearby river. At something like 4.00am the combination of flapping tent, howling wind, slippery ground and an urgent message from my bladder convinced me this was not a sensible exercise. Daylight, and with a chance to struggle back into warmer clothes, was welcome as never before.

On Sunday morning the site looked alarmingly like a refugee camp in some distant mountains, bleary eyed humans moving slowly through the mud as numerous Armstrong MT500s hinted at a military presence. Bikes ranging from a Brough Superior to the latest sports models picked their way along the road towards the exit as the horde headed for home. There were warm drinks in the tent intended for the band, and we supped a cup as weary club members collected huge plastic bags and set off to clear the site of rubbish. We thanked them for their efforts and endurance, waited for a flurry of snow to clear, kicked the Nortons into life and headed down the damp A5.

Bruce seemed keen to get home, the old single getting close to 60mph before it nipped up and we stopped for it to cool. Down the straight wastes of the A5 there was a clang-clanging down below from my bike, but I knew from experience it was a broken centre stand retaining spring. Mr Bungee to the rescue again. With a final wave our routes divided and I gave the Dominator its head, pulling out to overtake a line of crawlers on one of Shropshire's fine hills only to be slowed by a misfire.

I think it was telling me: " We're a bit long in the tooth for this boss." So never again, but let's talk in October, eh?

Written by Jim Reynolds for CBG

IT'S SNOW JOKE, IT'S THE DRAGON!

The Dragon 2007 weekend was upon us, and the club's contingent of representative sadists formed up for Breakfast at Steve's diner at Bedwas at a leisurely 8.00am. It was snowing, but forecast to stop, and the temperature was holding up above freezing-just.

There was three distinct groups this year, Road, trail and Sidecar. The road crew were Yoshi on his girlfriends 650 funduro, Springy on his pride & joy 900 Triumph adventurer and 17 year old Lewis doing his first rally on a 125 custom Suzuki.

Heavy snow makes going to the Dragon more of an adventure.

The Trail riders were Big Nige, Jason and Hermon- all KTM mounted, DRZ man Glyn and Russ Cosway on a Gas Gas 200-2 stroke. The odd-wheelers were Robin on his 40,000 mile 1978 MZ TS250 outfit and me on my 1991 Jawa TS350 / Velorex combination.

I planned a route for the road riders, which took in the ranges, Abergwesyn-Tregarron Pass, Devils Bridge, Nant-y-Moch reservoir and then a camp site in Dolgellau for the first night. From there a stroll through Snowdonia to the rally site on Anglesey. The return was to come down to Bala, then on some minor lanes to lake Vrynwy and B roads to Newtown before heading home via Builth and Brecon. Nige was leading the trail riders, and he had planned another megathon trail ride in typical big Nige style.

It all started well enough, everyone roaring off in anticipating a grand weekend. It didn't last long however as the snow got worse and showed no sign of letting up. It started to go decidedly pear shaped for the road and sidecar group about 25 miles from the start, the forecast of rain and a thaw, as is now widely known, was famously wrong, and the pass at Storey Arms was taken in blizzard conditions.

The A470 north towards Brecon got worse, and the planned route was now been seriously doubted by the road bike contingent due to the vast amount of snow falling from the sky and its tendency to stick around the roads. In the event, the road bike crew decided on a run up the A-roads leaving Robin and myself to run the gauntlet of the deteriorating weather on the original planned route along the more er-*scenic* roads! Yee Haaaa!

Geoffrey Fairhead travelling through the Llanberis Pass in heavy snow in 2007.

It was just like being a small boy again playing in the snow, the two of us sliding the outfits around like hooligans, overtaking ponderous 4x4's choosing the deepest snow and the narrowest un-gritted side roads we could find just for the hell of it! it was absolutely brilliant!

THE upper/lower Chapel Road had a couple of inches of lying snow, but it was quite grippy and the ruts in the snow went down to the tarmac.

When we got to the Garth turnoff however it all looked very different. The snow was getting deeper all the time, but the road up to the ranges looked positively arctic! A huge green 4x4 tractor came down the road and stopped by us "you're not intenin goin' up there are ya?" said the farmer from his heated cab, " it's bloody awful" I looked at Robin and knew instantly where we were going!

On the climb up to the Eppynt ranges it was surprising how much grip I got considering my standard Czechoslovakian rear road tyre, and with an East German off road type tyre on the rear of his MZ, Robin had no problems at all. I ended up at 90 degrees to the road and in a ditch once or twice, but that was possibly down to enthusiasm overwhelming ability! Robin's MZ ominously stuttered and coughed a bit so he changed the plug, but the problem was to return.

At the far end of the ranges the road was in virtual whiteout conditions, and Robin performed an enthusiastic pirouette as he slid over a frozen cattle grid.

The descent to Garth seemed easier than it looked, and as we were now tuned into the conditions we barrelled along the skating rink roads at a rapid rate. Steering had to be rethought as the front wheel had very little to do with the direction you ended up going. It was down to controlling things with the throttle. Accelerate to turn left, decelerate to turn right-easy!

At Bulah we fuelled up for the proposed trek over the Tregaron Pass, surprisingly the Jawa 350 twin was proving far more frugal on the juice than the increasingly sick sounding MZ. Five miles later on a toboggan run of road leading to Abergwesyn the MZ quit again.

After liberally spraying everything in sight with aircraft spec. WD40 Robin decided that he needed to keep the bike on the boil to stop it choking up, as his usual riding style is at the top end of the throttle range, chugging along in the snow he figured, was oiling up the plug-or something!

The net result of this line of thought was a prolonged session of flat out sidecar tomfoolery in the snow! I tried in vain to keep the rear of the MZ outfit in sight as we broadsided around sharp bends, used ditches and bankings for braking and slingshotting around the most ridiculous downhill s-bends on roads that are best described as pistes! I looked at my speedo on one occasion to see the needle above the 45mph mark at the top of a ridge with a downhill right hander in front of me. I stuffed it into the banking to lose some speed and somehow got around, Robin, by now had long gone!

Eventually we reached Abergwesyn and the Tregaron road. This was deep snow. There was possibly two feet of soft snow on top of an icy surface. It took me about 45 minutes to get 100 meters up the road, Robin had slithered ahead, his special East German snow tyre doing the business for the grip.

HE returned some time later unable to progress to the foot of the Devil's Staircase, and as going up the Devil's Staircase was out of the question without a Chinook we decided to give the Tregaron Pass a miss.

Back on the A roads the conditions were only slightly better, but before long Robin pulled over with a sick sounding engine. This time however the problem was sussed, the carb looked twice it's normal size as it now had a nice jacket of ice! It looked like the problem all along was down to carb icing. Robin sacrificed his first choice gloves and tie wrapped them to the carb hoping that they would stop it freezing. In the end it helped, but unlike the Jawa, the MZ still suffered in the worst conditions. One up for Czechoslovakia!

The road from Llandovery to Lampeter was fantastic! The ice and snow, lack of traffic and wide road made for extreme fun. Left handers were the best for me, go in at a steady speed and whack the throttle open as you enter the corner, the outfit slews sideways and goes round as if on rails. Right handers had to be taken on a dead throttle or shut off, and using the ruts as berms. As Robin's German outfit is on the right the technique is the opposite.

The Jawa on route to the Dragon

We eventually got to Tregaron and stopped for a hot chocolate. It hadn't stopped snowing all day and the roads, even the A roads, were getting worse. In the event we decided on a detour to Machynlleth to meet up with the trail riders before deciding if we were going to make it to the campsite. Aberystwyth was bathed in sunshine! The roads were dry and the only snow around was the snow that still clung onto the sidecar frames-and, of course Robin's carb! The difference was amazing. People getting out of their cars at the petrol station were in tee-shirts whilst no more than 30 miles up the road survival suits were the de-rigour attire!

We headed back up the A roads to Machynlleth with darkness falling with the temperature.

At the White Lion we were surprised not to see the trail bikes around the back, and even more surprised to receive a call from Jason telling us that they had turned around just outside Brecon unable to progress on the off-road route. They were giving this year's Dragon a miss. Yoshi and the road bikes had got as far as Llandovery and had found a warm pub to hole up in until the next day. Robin and myself considered pushing on to Dolgellau and the camp site just 15 miles up the road, but the lure of a warm pub and hot grub was to much so we stayed in the White Lion.

I was fairly Knackered by then anyway, and a good meal and a good night's sleep were definitely required. The meal was crap (unusually, because last year it was quite good) and I couldn't sleep for the aching in my shoulders from heaving the outfit around on the snow. However, that's a small price to well worth paying for such a fantastic day!

Saturday's ride started at 10.00am, we had plenty of time as we only had to chug up over Snowdonia. I took time to repair my steering damper, which had dismantled itself during the run up, and Robin bought some meths.

HE reckons it was to put in the tank to stop the petrol from freezing in the carb, but I never saw any go in the tank.....Ya never can tell with these Rogerstone types!

The run around Lake Bala and the road over Rhyd was absolutely spectacular, but as usual Snowdon was clagged in. I reckon that if the government wanted to put a top secret site anywhere, then the top of mount Snowdon would be perfect. It's hardly ever seen! There could be a great open air nuclear missile site there and nobody would ever know-since all you ever see up there is inside of a cloud!

Anglesey however, arrived in perfect sunshine and blue skies. You had to look across the Menai Straits at the heavy clouds around Snowdon to remind ourselves of the weather we rode through the past couple of days. If you arrived there from the air you'd think it was a mid-spring day not a wintry weekend in early February.

At the campsite I was surprised to see Yoshi, Springy endlessly riding towards us. I had figured that being snowed in all day at the pub would have seen the inevitable result of inebriation and they'd head home with a hangover on the Saturday. But motor power to their elbow, they were up early took advantage of the clear A roads and got to Anglesey before us.

The mistake they made was to pitch tents right outside the main hall where the band played, and right next to the makeshift urinal eu natural!

Rod Morgan's Honda on the way to the Dragon through the Llanberis Pass.

Robin spotted some MZ-ers and we pitched tents at a sensible distance from the mayhem. The rally itself was more or less as it was the previous year, that is you drink, you listen to the band trying to play with the acoustics of an aircraft hanger to contend with, eat whatever you brought, and try and sleep in a tent in the rain.

I bumped into the man with 6mm nuts in his beard-Mike Fry, and Gary Slippers etc. lots of MZ, sidecar and Jawa related talk, all in all a pleasant time was had by all. All that is, except Yoshi, Springy and Lewis, who had the meaty whiff of 1000 bloke's piss to accompany their attempt at slumber, a band that played sporadically until 4.00am and a car boot sale that used the hall and began to arrive at 5.00am!! Oh and it rained all night too.

They slept well-not!

After packing up, the Sundays ride started out in sunshine, but as the previous day had seen us tackle every possible type of weather available, I took the precaution of wearing waterproofs. They weren't needed and the run home was exactly as planned, and more or less dry. We passed the old traditional Dragon Rally site near Betws-y-Coed on the A5, and it looked bleak! According to Robin the nearest pub had been built onto the side of a cliff face, complete with run-off water through the lounge. The party trick was to get pissed and see how far up the cliff you could climb before falling-and probably breaking your neck to the sound of drunken cheering! Hmm, good ole days?

BY the time we got to Bala the winter scenes had returned again and the minor roads were almost as bad as they were on Friday. On one single-track pass to the south west of Lake Vrynwy and with a huge un-barriered drop to the right, and an icy snow covered road we came across a Land Rover coming down the steep climb towards us. Robin was in front and stopped, the driver of the Land Rover put his brakes on, the wheels locked and the big 4x4 just carried on coming like a 1 ton toboggan! The drivers eyes were as big as saucers as he realised he was actually a passenger and Robin and I furiously paddled backwards down this icy climb with the bairrier-less drop off looming on the right.

Eventually we reversed to a place where we could go into the ditch on the left and let the farmer and his out of control Land Rover get past us.

The B-roads we took from Llanfair Caereinion to Newtown were tremendous and by the time we reached Llandrindod I was suffering from nice-benditis! Outfits are fantastic fun on the road, you can be outrageously hairy at quite sensible speeds, and accelerating out of a left hander with the chair wheel a couple of feet in the air wasn't unusal.

From Llandod we went over Hundred House and down onto the Brecon road and home over Storey Arms.

We covered a tad under 500 miles on the outfits and only had to make a minor detour from my original plan. The weekend is one for the books, the weather played a huge part in the enjoyment for me, and it fitted in perfectly with my recent conversion to three wheels, and convinced me of the attraction of the sidecar.

Written by Paul Lear

The weather was almost like a spring day at the Anglesey Dragon site,
Completely different from the snow storms encountered inland on the way.

THE DRAGON, I FEAR NOT?

After the hardest winter for over 20 years, I had to admit I was slightly dubious about camping out at the Dragon Rally. But my husband convinced me that after two years of him riding through snow to the Dragon they're surely wouldn't be a third. It snowed heavy the weekend before the Dragon, I was not amused.

So I prepared myself for cold weather, by purchasing plenty of warm gear and a pair of very fetching long-johns. I only usually go pillion in the summer, so this was definitely an adventure for me.

On the way to the Dragon, just after collecting our entry tickets from the control caravan.

On the morning of the Dragon ,the weather had thankfully improved. It was dry, clear and frosty. Me and my husband, Rod, set off on his Honda CX500 and our friend John travelled on his Yamaha XV750.

The Journey to the A5 was smooth and enjoyable, but it was very cold and I began to lose feeling in my feet and hands. I'm not a very warm blooded creature, show me a woman who doesn't suffer from cold feet and hands, at the best of times! So I was beginning to feel like I needed a stop just to get the circulation going again. But first we had to go through Llangollen and then we had a stop at Corwen for a bacon buttie and a hot cup of tea.

After warming up a tad we had to go on the diversion at Corwen, due to part of the A5 been shut, so over to Bala we headed through freezing fog and some very treacherous black ice on the roads. When we came down into Betws-y-Coed we started meeting up with fellow Dragon Rallyists, and all headed off to the control Caravan, which was situated on the B5106 by Tal-y-Bont.

Dragon Rallyists entering the first part of the site up to the marquee

We chatted with some fellow Dragonists, a couple of them, who hadn't brought any camping gear with them, were planning on drinking plenty and kipping any where they could for the night!

We found the turning to Rowen and headed into the rally site, which was situated in some woods. At first we thought we would stay in the wooded section, but we went on up to the marquee and saw there was a top field, and we pitched there for the night. We went down to collect our goodie bags, soup and badge from the marquee, met Ken Davies, from the Conwy MCC. And watched other rallyists arriving.

When we went back to the tents I was introduced to Jerry Frantz ,who comes from Luxembourg, and is a well know Dragon Rallyist. I proceeded to lose my husband and John to the 'bike talking fraternity', so I sat on my hay bale and watched the bikes arrive on site.

WHILE we watched people arriving, on a huge assortment of bikes and sidecars, a Honda Goldwing got stuck in some mud at the beginning of the field. He locked his front brake and with the throttle open, while still holding the brake, he let the clutch out and it ploughed towards the crowd of people opposite us and knocked a BMW right over. Fortunately nobody was hurt and the rider most probably suffered more damage to his pride than the damage to both bikes. A few expletives filled the air but all was soon sorted out.

We decided to visit one of the pubs, there was one in Rowen and another towards the main road. We chose the one in Rowen. It was a beautiful clear crisp evening and there were small camp fires burning all through the wood, where rallyists were cooking food and keeping warm. The pub in Rowen was packed and full of rallyists enjoying themselves and telling stories about other Dragon rallies.

Kenny Davies from the Conwy M.C.C and a colleague with Rod and John.

We spent a great evening there and we did plan to head back to the marquee to listen to the band, but the pub was warm and comfortable with plenty of drink left. In fact we were the last rallyists to leave the pub after midnight.

By this time a hard frost was developing and the alcohol was taking a bit more of an effect on me than I anticipated.

After a bit of food we headed to the tents up the hill and noticed that the now muddy hill was beginning to freeze-not good.

Sleep was very hard to find as the amount of snoring, odd shouting and other male bodily noises was hard to ignore. Plus a strange crackling noise, which we found out in the morning was the ice on the inside of our tent!

We were rudely awoken at 6.00 am by John, of all people, packing up his gear and rattling pans. One rallyists near us, who was also woken by John, shouted out " Hey mate you must teach me how to get a tent down in the dark!" He wasn't the only one annoyed.

So we decided to get up too. I was very cold due to my darling husband sitting on my hand warmer the night before and putting it out, due to my inebriated state I was unable to relight it. A cold woman is not one to be bargained with or spoken to unless you want your head bitten off ! There had been a hard frost and everything looked frozen, including me. By now rallyists were starting to wake up and have breakfast.

A fair few bikes would not start due to frozen chokes, oil thickening and loss of power in batteries, due to the temperature.

The toilets were in quite a state due to the water been frozen and some of the Conwy Club members were desperately trying to sort it out.

It needed a small nuclear explosion to get that moving and get rid of what was in the mens toilets, according to my husband.

The hard frost that greeted us at sunrise Brrrrr!

WE then began to realise that it might have been a good idea to camp down in the wood, as one-we wouldn't of got as cold, two-we could have had a fire, then three-we wouldn't of had the hill to tackle. While I went to the toilet I watched some of the bikes trying to tackle the now very slippy, muddy and icy bank. It needed a fair amount of skill to get down with out sliding as one biker discovered, he ended up in the hedge with his bike on top of him, with the bike still running, so I went to his aid ,with another rallyist, who turned the bike off before helping the rallyist up, unfortunately his fairing had suffered damage, but at least he hadn't sustained any injuries.

I told my husband and John about the conditions of the bank, and a few others around us, we immediately packed up knowing that once more bikes got on it the worse it would become. They both made it safely down the bank.

We said our good-byes to Kenny and other members of the Conwy Club, avoided the local Police, who were sniffing around, and got ready to head for home.

I was too frozen to remember much of the journey, but it was a clear, frosty morning with just the odd bank of fog lingering here and there.

I was so pleased to get home as I felt like a frozen zombie, but at least I did the Dragon Rally.

Rod and the CX defrosting slowly.

Will I do it again? For some unknown reason that I cant explain, Yes I will! It was an experience that I will never forget, and it somehow makes you feel very alive, and makes you wander if you are totally mad camping out in a frozen field in -5 in the middle of winter, but The Dragon draws you into its lair, holds you captive, then gently lets you go, only to lure you back the next year.

See you all soon.

Written By Carol Morgan

Kenny Davies (Left) and Johnny Emms (right). Who Sadly passed away in 2009. Johnny Emms was a well know character and entertained many people at the Dragon rallies over the years. And let everyone know when he was appearing on Eastenders! He always showed his support of the Dragon Rally by wearing a badge or T-shirt on screen.

A John Emms Memorial Trophy was kindly presented to the Conwy M.C.C by Mrs Margaret Emms, which will be awarded every year to loyal supporters of the Dragon Rally.

This year it was awarded to Maurice Kettle, a Honda enthusiast, who has attended all 49 rallies.

A COPY OF THE DRAGON RALLY SONGBOOK 1965

Greetings, Dragonists,

Once again the Conway Club welcomes all of you; you who have been with us at Bryn Bras and at Gwyrich and all those who are trying wintery North Wales for the first time. And especially welcome are you who crossed the sea to be with us. Bonjour and Guten Tag.

Those of you who were at the first of the rallies will know this place — it is Llyn Padarn — virtually next door to Bryn Bras in Llanberis. The ride to Gwyrich was getting too easy for you all! We'll see what the Pen y pas covered in ice can do to you.

May we as President and Chairman take this opportunity to thank all those who have done so much to make this rally possible — the owners of the site, the rank and file of the Conway Club who did most of the hard graft, Harry Louis and John Ebbrol and the rest of the Motor Cycle staff, Bill Hume — our Geordie Conway Club member from darkest Sunderland! — and Messrs. B.S.A. who compiled and published this song sheet for us, Bill Thacker who created the Dragon and drew the cover for us — free! — our lady members for the soup and their work, everybody who did any work at all in fact.

But the work of the Dragon Rally isn't over when you all stagger off home — not by any means. We have the rubbish *YOU* leave behind to clear up. So let us include our thanks to you, my Dragon Rallying friend, because you rode off home taking your tins, your cigarette packets, your paper bags and your assorted junk, rubbish and trash with you. *If* you must be a litter lout — camp in your own flipping garden.

So have a good ride up — or down. Have a good time here. Make new friends and greet old ones. Let the camp fire blaze again. It's a great, great time we have together. The effort is worth it all.

'PIP' HARRIS (*President*),
BRYN THOMAS (*Chairman*),
Conway and District Motor Cycle Club.

THE DRAGON RALLY 1965

SONG SHEET

compiled by

Bill Hume

(*Conway & District M.C.C. & The Vintage Motor Cycle Club*)

The Conway Club would like to thank

BSA

MOTOR CYCLES LTD.

for their great generosity in bearing the costs of having this publication printed.

The Conway & District Motor Cycle Club

SONG OF THE DRAGON MEN

Hear! The sound in valleys ringing
  With the motors' raucous singing,
As again machines are winging
  Onward into Wales!
Wide the throttle — engine's growling
  Mingling with the wild wind's howling.
It echoes from the grey crags scowling
  On the way to Wales.

  Onward to the meeting!
    Warm will be the greeting!
  Let it blow! Come sleet! Come snow!
    Who cares a damn about the winter
        weather?
  Swiftly, smoothly, wheels are turning.
    To our fore a beacon's burning.
  Down remembered roads returning.
    Dragons into Wales!

Let who dare not, stay behind us
  Crouched by firesides: they'll not
      find us.
Warmth and comfort do not bind us.
  Call us then insane!
Hillsides whisper — we can't dally.
  Hear the sound sweep down the valley!
Wheels to Wales! Wheels to the Rally!
  Hear the call again!

  Through the winter snow, men!
    Dragons all! We go men!
  Let it blow! Come sleet! Come snow!
    Who cares a damn about the winter
        weather?
  Wild as wind the mountains seeking
    From the towns where smoke hangs
        reeking
  Cymru calls us! Hear her speaking!
    We will meet again.

Bill Hume and Ron Miller

2. *DID YOU EVER SEE?*

Now the Dragon's held in Wales where they drink their beer from pails?
If you want a pint on Sunday, man, you'll have to wait 'till Monday.
Did you ever see? Did you ever saw? Did you ever see such a funny thing before?

Now my maiden Aunt Amantha has come down upon her Panther.
My she looks so sweet and inn'cent. You should see her on her Vincent!
Did you ever see? Did you ever saw? Did you ever see such a funny thing before?

I came on a Brough bright red. "'Tis a museum piece!" they said.
The poor brute now is pantin' — but she's left the others stantin'.
Did you ever see? Did you ever saw? Did you ever see such a funny thing before?

On a bike of Enfield make coming down by Bala Lake.
My friend Freddie's sidecar lifted. From the saddle bricks we shifted!
Did you ever see? Did you ever saw? Did you ever see such a funny thing before?

On the Bwlch y Groes I got on a two-stroke — it was a Cotton.
As they said I'd have no bother — but Oh Cripes I want my mother!
Did you ever see? Did you ever saw? Did you ever see such a funny thing before?

I've a little sister Dot, she came down upon her Scott.
But it seized! She should have orter filled that grid thing up with water.
Did you ever see? Did you ever saw? Did you ever see such a funny thing before?

Johnny went and came a cropper when he clobbered that big copper.
To his Triumph he wrote "Finis!" for his tax disc's blazoned "Guinness".
Did you ever see? Did you ever saw? Did you ever see such a funny thing before?

Once he used to smoke cigars. Now a B.M. Steib now has.
'Bout his plot he shoots the big lines — but he now is smoking Woodbines.
Did you ever see? Did you ever saw? Did you ever see such a funny thing before?

Now a Jawa I am certain's from behind the iron curtain.
In the tool box there's a lickle iron hammer and a sickle.
Did you ever see? Did you ever saw? Did you ever see such a funny thing before?

Into Anglesey Sam rode. How he got there no one knowed.
He had piston slap and big-end knock. It died in Llanfairpwyllgwyngyllgogerychwrynllantisilio-gogogoch.
Did you ever see? Did you ever saw? Did you ever see such a funny thing before?

I came off an Atlas Norton not long after I had gort on.
But they laughed. It looked so farcial, for I skated on my elbow.
Did you ever see? Did you ever saw? Did you ever see such a funny thing before?

Lordy! How he cut a dash on his Beeza Golden Flash.
But he's quiet now — not rantin! He was towed in by a Bantam.
Did you ever see? Did you ever saw? Did you ever see such a funny thing before?

To the Rally on a Raleigh. By the road he didn't dally.
He has earned his Dragon Medal for he came down using pedals.
Did you ever see? Did you ever saw? Did you ever see such a funny thing before?

Now my friend a Velo fellow met a lush piece and said "Hallo".
Now his four kids can say "Dadda" and his Viper—well he's adder.
Did you ever see? Did you ever saw? Did you ever see such a funny thing before?

On a Honda my friend Ron, bet that he could reach the ton.
How he looks so neat and tidy. See you at the church on Friday.
Did you ever see? Did you ever saw? Did you ever see such a funny thing before?

Droopy bars and a rev dial, Oscar eats mile after mial.
Makes the motorists look sickly as he bombs by — on his Quickly.
Did you ever see? Did you ever saw? Did you ever see such a funny thing before?

Now a Yank a Harley brought of the customerised sort.
But she's quite a job I'm thinkin'. The left pannier's got the sink in.
Did you ever see? Did you ever saw? Did you ever see such a funny thing before?

Now a change is like a rest and though I like the Matchless best.
I will put cash by each pay day and I'll get myself an — Ayjay!
Did you ever see? Did you ever saw? Did you ever see such a funny thing before?

So into Wales we rode on, 'till at last we came to Snowdon.
But the road sign's writing's Rhondda. That's a slag heap over yonder.
Did you ever see? Did you ever saw? Did you ever see such a funny thing before?

As a map reader he's lousy — or he must be feeling drowsy.
For he says Montgomery we're in but that sign says — Sir Dryfaldwyn.
Did you ever see? Did you ever saw? Did you ever see such a funny thing before?

Tommy boy's a Dragon Lad. Like us others raving mad.
And I'll swear he does the Dragon just to spend the whole year braggon.
Did you ever see? Did you ever saw? Did you ever see such a funny thing before?

Bill Hume

3. *THE SONG OF THE ELEPHANT MEN*

(*to the tune of "High Barbaree"*)

Now that the New Year's come, to the Nurnburgring we run.
Blow high! Blow low! And so ride we!
Through the swirling snow flakes and the watery winter sun.
A-riding and a-roving like the wandering wind we're free!

Blow high! Blow low! And so ride we!
A-riding and a-roving like the wandering wind we're free!

The land is white with snow-drifts and the cold wind howls its song.
But to the road! — the open road! — for that's where we belong.

To the camp-fire's crackle where the cosy tent's a home.
And there we'll yarn. There's friendship born and we'll be meeting soon.

Bill Hume

4. *THE BIG ROCK CANDY MOUNTAIN*

On a summer's day in the month of May a burly bum came hiking
Down a shady lane by the sugar cane; he was looking for his liking.
He sang a song of a land so gay, a land of milk and honey.
Where a bum can stay for many a day and you don't need any money.

Oh, the buzzin' of the bees in the cigarette trees
And the soda water fountains
Where the lemonade springs and the bluebird sings
In the Big Rock Candy Mountain.

In that Big Rock Candy Mountain all the cops have wooden legs,
The bulldogs all have rubber teeth and the hens lay soft boiled eggs,
The farmer's trees are full of fruit. Their barns are full of hay.
I want to go where there ain't no snow
And the sleet don't fall and the wind don't blow
And a bum can sleep all day.

In that Big Rock Candy Mountain you never change your socks
And the little streams of alcohol come trickling down the rocks;
The shacks all have to tip their hats and the railroad bulls are blind,
There's a lake of stew and of whisky too,
You can paddle around in a big canoe
In that Big Rock Candy Mountain.

5. *GREEN GROW THE RUSHES*

I'll give you one O!
Green grow the rushes O!
What is your one O?
One is one and all alone and ever more shall be so.

Two, two, the lily white boys clothed all in green o-ho!

Three, three the rivals.

Four for the gospel makers.

Five for the symbols at your door.

Six for the six proud walkers.

Seven for the seven bright stars in the sky.

Eight for the April rainers.

Nine for the nine bright shiners.

Ten for the ten commandments.

Eleven for the eleven who went to heaven.

Twelve for the twelve apostles.

6. *SHE WAS POOR BUT SHE WAS HONEST*

She was poor but she was honest, victim of a Squire's whim.
First he loved her then he left her. Isn't it a flippin' shame?

So she ran away to London for to hide her grief and shame;
There she met a ton-up wonder and she lost her name again.

See him riding on his Goldy, past the gutter where she stands,
He has wed a dealer's daughter and she wrings her ringless hands.

See him in a transport cafe by the juke box with the best
While the girl what he has ruined entertains a sordid guest.

See her on the bridge at midnight, saying "Farewell, blighted love!"
Then a scream, a splash, good heavens, what is she a-doing of?

When they dragged her from the river, water from her clothes they rung;
Though they thought that she was drownded still her corpse got up and sung.

In a lowly little cottage where her aged parents live;
They drink the Champagne that she sends them but they never can forgive.

It's the same the whole world over, it's the poor wot gets the blame;
It's the rich wot gets the gravy, isn't it a blooming shame?

Sad! Let's cheer up!

7. *GLORIOUS BEER*

Beer, beer, glorious beer! Fill yourself right up to here!
Drink a good deal of it, make a big meal of it,
Stick to your old fashioned beer!
Don't be afraid of it, drink till you're made of it,
Let's put another down here!
Up with the sale of it, down with a pail of it,
Glorious, glorious beer!

(and another chorus!)

8. *I WANNA GO HOME*

We sailed on the old John Dee, my grandpappy and me
For over the Seven Seas we wanted to roam.
But we're fightin' all day and we're drinkin' all night.
I feel so break up, I wanna go home.
So hist up the big main sail.
And pull up the anchor chain.
And put down your helm and head her over the foam.
I wanna go home!
I wanna go home!
I feel so break up
I wanna go home!

The Master's a wicked man, he gets drunk every time he can.
He don't give a damn about grandpappy and me.
He knocks us about and he kicks us around.
I feel so break up, I wanna go home.

9. *ONE EYED RILEY*

As I was sitting by Riley's fire, drinking Riley's rum and water,
Suddenly a thought came to my head, I'd like to marry old Riley's daughter.

Rub-a-dub dub! Rub-a-dub dub!
Rub-a-dub dub for the one-eyed Riley!
Yippy-aye-ay! Yippee-aye-ay!
Yippy-aye-ay! Trez bon.

Her hair was black and her eyes were blue; the colonel and the major and the captain sought her,
The sergeant and the private and the drummer boy too, but they never had a chance with the Riley's daughter.

Riley played on the big bass drum; Riley had a mind full of murder and slaughter.
Riley had one big bright red eye and he kept that eye on his lovely daughter.

I got me a ring and a parson too and I grabbed me a scratch in the married quarter;
Settled me down to a peaceful life happy as a king with the Riley's daughter.

Suddenly a footstep on the stairs. Who should it be but the one-eyed Riley,
He had two pistols in his hand. He was looking for the man who married his daughter.

I grabbed old Riley by the leg and stuffed his head in a bucket of water.
Fired his pistols in the air, a darned sight quicker than I married his daughter.

(And stick to this version please!)

10. *WALTZING MATILDA*

Once a jolly swagman camped by a Billabong
  Under the shade of a Coolibah Tree.
And he sang as he sat and waited till his billy boiled.
  You'll come a Waltzing Matilda with me.

    Waltzing Matilda! Waltzing Matilda!
    You'll come a Waltzing Matilda with me.
    And he sang as he sat and waited till his billy boiled.
    You'll come a Waltzing Matilda with me.

Up came a jumbuck to drink at the Billabong
  Up jumped the swagman and grabbed he with glee.
And he sang as he stuffed that jumbuck in his tucker bag.
  You'll come a Waltzing Matilda with me.

Up came the squatter mounted on his thoroughbred
  Up came the troopers, one, two, three.
"Oh where's the jolly jumbuck, you've got in your tucker bag?"
  You'll come a Waltzing Matilda with me.

Up jumped the swagman and sprang into the Billabong,
  "You'll never take me alive!" says he.
And his ghost may be heard if you walk by that Billabong,
  You'll come a Waltzing Matilda with me.

11. *THE MAD MOTOR-CYCLIST*

A mad motor-cyclist lay dying—(dying)
  At the end of a new motorway
His oppoes were gathered around him—(round him)
  To carry the pieces away.
The engine was curved round his wishbone
  The footrest was wrapped round his head
A spark plug stuck from his left ear 'ole
  'Twas plain that he'd shortly be dead.

He spat out a valve and a gasket—(gasket)
  He stirred in the frame where he lay.
And they eased both the forks and wheel off him—(off him)
  Then these last parting words he did say.
"Take the push rods from out of my larynx
  And the sprocket from out of my brain
The timing case take from my kidneys.
  And assemble the engine again."

"The piston I think's in my stomach—(stomach)
  The damper is stuck in my neck,
Extract from my liver the con-rod—(con-rod),
  There's a stack of good parts in the wreck.
I'll be riding a cloud in the morning
  With a harp not a throttle to hold
Where the tappets do not need adjusting
  Way behind those tall gates chrome and gold."

Bill Hume

12. *ABDUL EL BULBUL EMIR*

The sons of the prophet were brave men and bold
  And quite unaccustomed to fear.
But the bravest by far in the ranks of the Shah
  Was Abdul el Bulbul Emir.
If you wanted a man to encourage the van
  Or to harass the foe from the rear.
Storm fort or redoubt you had only to shout
  For Abdul el Bulbul Emir.

There were heroes in plenty and well known to fame
  In the ranks that were led by the Tsar,
But none had more fame than a man of the name
  Of Ivan Skavinsky Skivar.
He could sing like Bing Crosby and Old Sachmo too
  And strum an electric guitar
In fact quite the cream of the Muscovite team
  Was Ivan Skavinsky Skivar.

One day this bold Russian had shouldered his gun
  And donned his most truculent sneer.
Down town did he go and he trod on the toe
  Of Abdul el Bulbul Emir.
"Young man" quoth Abdul, "Has life grown so dull
  That you wish to end your career?"
Vile infidel, know, you have trod on the toe
  Of Abdul el Bulbul Emir."

So take your last look at the sunshine and brook.
  And send your regrets to the Tsar;
By this I imply you are going to die,
  Count Ivan Skavinsky Skivar!"
Said Ivan, "My friend, your remarks in the end
  Will avail you but little I fear.
You ne'er will survive to repeat them alive
  Mr. Abdul el Bulbul Emir!"

Then the bold Mameluke drew his trusty skibouk
  And crying out "Allah Akbar!"
With murderous intent he ferociously went
  For Ivan Skavinsky Skivar.
They fought all that night neath the pale Tartar moon,
  The din it was heard from afar.
Vast multitudes came so great was the fame
  Of Abdul and Ivan Skivar.

As Abdul's long knife was extracting the life
  (In fact he was shouting "Huzza!")
He felt himself struck by that wily Kalmuck
  Count Ivan Skavinsky Skivar.
The Sultan approached in his Rolls Silver Ghost
  Expecting the victor to cheer
He arrived just in time to exchange a last line
  With Abdul el Bulbul Emir.

Tsar Petrovitch too in his spectacles blue.
  Drove past in his Mercedes car
But he only drew nigh to hear the last sigh
  Of Ivan Skavinsky Skavar.
A Muscovite maiden her lone vigil keeps
  'Neath the light of the pale polar star
And the name that she murmurs so oft as she weeps
  Is Ivan Skavinsky Skivar.

A tomb rises up where the Blue Danube rolls.
  Carved on it in characters clear
Are "Stranger, when passing, Oh pray for the soul
  Of Abdul el Bulbul Emir".
A splash in the Black Sea one dark moonless night
  Caused ripples to spread wide and far.
'Twas made by a sack fitting close to the back
  Of Ivan Skavinsky Skivar!

13. *THE BLUE TAILED FLY*

When I was young I used to wait upon the boss and pass his plate.
And pass the bottle when he got dry — and brush away the blue tailed fly.

Gimmee crack corn and I don't care.
Gimmee crack corn and I don't care.
Gimmee crack corn and I don't care.
The master's gone away.

And when he'd ride in the afternoon I'd follow on with a hickory broom;
The pony it was rather shy when bitten by the blue tailed fly.

The day he rode around the farm, the flies were numerous and did swarm.
One chanced to bite him on the thigh; the devil take that blue tailed fly.

The Pony run, he jump, he pitch. He flung the master into a ditch;
He died, the jury wondered why — the verdict was the blue tailed fly.

They lay him 'neath a 'simmon tree. The epitaph is there to see.
"Beneath this grave I'm forced to lie a victim of the blue tailed fly.

14. *THE DARKIES' SUNDAY SCHOOL*

Old folk, young folk everybody come.
Join our darkies' Sunday School and make yourself at home.
Bring your sticks of chewing gum and sit upon the floor
And we'll tell you Bible stories that you've never heard before.

Adam was the first man, that's what we all believe,
  'Til one day he was filleted, and introduced to Eve.
He had no one to tell him but he soon found out the way
  And that's the only reason why we're sitting here today.

Now Adam was a gardener with Eve his gentle spouse
  They got the sack for stealing fruit and took to keeping cows
Life was very peaceful — 'twas quiet in the main
  Until they had a baby boy and started raising Cain.

Mr. Lot and Mrs. Lot went out for a stroll
  Sodom got too hot and so they left the rotten hole;
Mrs. Lot turned herself round to go and fetch her jacket
  Now she sold as Saxa salt at sevenpence a packet.

Esau was a cowboy from the wild and woolly west,
  His daddy left him half the ranch and Brother Jake the rest;
But Esau thought the title deeds were very far from clear
  So he sold the whole caboodle for a sandwich and a beer.

Pharoah's daughter Miriam went walking by the Nile
  Found the infant Moses playing with a crocodile;
She took him home to father said she'd found him on the shore,
  But Pharoah slying winked at her, he'd heard that one before.

Moses was the leader of the Israelitish flock
  And when the flock was thirsty he just struck upon the rock
And when the rock was opened there arose a mighty cheer
  For instead of flowing water there was found a well of beer.

David was a general, Uriah was sub.
  David saw Uriah's wife when she was in her tub
David sent Uriah off to scout a front line trench
  Uriah got a hand grenade and David got the wench.

Elishah was a prophet and his head was rather bare—
  The children shouted "Shiny Top! Why don't you cut your hair?"
This angered old Elishah so he called his brindled pup
  Which being fond of children — ate the little baskets up.

Shadrach was a prophet who was chucked into the fire
  Expected by the stoker to immediately expire.
But when they opened the furnace up, the asbestos laddie laughed.
  And said "Me hinnies keep it shut. Aa cannot stand the draught!"

15. *FOGGY FOGGY DEW*

I was a bachelor, I lived by myself and I worked at the weavers trade
And the only thing I ever did wrong was to woo a fair young maid.
I wooed her in the Winter time and in the Summer too.
And the only, only thing that I ever did wrong was to keep her from the foggy, foggy dew.

One night she came to my bedside as I lay fast asleep.
She laid her pretty head upon my bed and she began to weep
She sighed, she cried, she damn near died. What was a man to do?
So I took her into bed and I covered up her head just to save her from the foggy, foggy dew.

Now I am a bachelor, I live with my son and we work at the weaver's trade
And every, every time I look into his eyes he reminds me of that fair young maid.
He reminds me in the Wintertime and in the Summer too,
And the many, many times that I held her in my arms just to save her from the foggy, foggy dew.

16. *ON TOP OF OLD SMOKEY*

On top of old Smokey all covered in snow,
I lost my true lover, from courting too slow.

Now courting's a pleasure and parting's a grief
And a false hearted lover is worth than a thief.

A thief will just rob you and take what you have
But a false hearted lover will be digging your grave.

The grave will decay you and turn you to dust,
There's no girl in a million a poor bloke can trust.

She'll tell you she loves you and tell you more lies
Than the cross ties on a railroad or stars in the sky.

Come all you young maidens and listen to me
Ne'er hang your affections on a green willow tree.

The leaves they will wither, the roots they will die
Your lover will leave you and you'll never know why.

17. *MY FAMILY*
(*Tune—My Bonny lies over the ocean*)

My father makes counterfeit money,
My mother brews synthetic gin,
My sister sells kisses to sailors,
By jove how the money rolls in.

Rolls in!
Rolls in!
By Jove how the money rolls in — rolls in!
Rolls in! Rolls in!
By Jove how the money rolls in.

My brother's a slum missionary,
Saving young ladies from sin.
He'll save you a blond for a shilling.
By Jove, how the money rolls in.

My aunt keeps a girl's seminary
Teaching young girls to begin.
She doesn't say where they're to finish!
By Jove how the money rolls in!

My cousin's a medical student,
With instruments long, sharp and thin.
He can only do one operation—
By Jove how the money rolls in!

I've spent all my counterfeit money,
I've guzzled the synthetic gin,
I've parted with my only shilling,
Oh hell what a state I am in!

18. *SOSPAN FACH*
(*This'll baffle the lot of you — Welshmen included*)

Mas bys Mari Ann wedi brifo
A Dafydd gwas ddim yn iach,
Mae'r baban yn y crud yn crio
A'r gath wedi scrapo Sioni bach.

Sospan fach yn berwi ar y tan
Sospan fawr yn berwi ar y llawr
A'r gath wedi scrapo Sioni bach.

Dai Bach y Soldiwr, Dai Bach y Soldiwr.
A chwt ei chrys y maes.
Sut chrys oedd gandde Sut chrys oedde gandde?
Crys bach gwyn a stripen las. Crys bach gwyn a stripen las.

Mae bys Nari Ann wedi gwella,
A Dafydd y Gwas yn ei fedd,
Mae'r baban yn y crud wedi twei,
A'r gath wedi huno mewn hedd.

19. *SWEET VIOLETS*

There once was a farmer who took a young Miss
In back of a barn where he gave her a
Lecture on horses and chickens and eggs
And told her that she had such beautiful
Manners that suited a girl of her charms
A girl that he wanted to take in his
Washing and ironing and then if she did
They could get married and raise lots of
Sweet violets, sweeter than all the roses
Covered all over from head to toe,
Covered all over in sweet violets.

The girl told the farmer that he'd better stop
Then she called her father and he called a
Taxi and got there before very long
Someone was doing his little girl
Right for a change and so that's why he said
"If you marry her, Son, you're better off
Single, for it's been my belief
Marriage can bring a man nothing but
Sweet violets. . . .

The farmer decided he'd wed anyway
And started in planning for his wedding
Suit, which he'd purchased for only one buck
Then he did find he was clean out of
Money and so he was left in the lurch
Standing there waiting in front of the
End of this story which just goes to show
All a girl wants from a man is his
Sweet violets. . . .

20. *THE WHIFFENPOOF SONG*

To the tables down at Mory's
To the place where Louis dwells,
To the dear old Temple Bar we loved so well,
See the Whiffenpoofs assembled
With their glasses raised on high
And the magic of their singing casts a spell.
Yes, the magic of their singing
Of the songs we loved so well
"Shall I Wasting" and "Mavourneen" and the rest;
We will seranade our Louis whilst life and voice shall last
Then we'll pass and be forgotten like the rest.

We're poor little lambs who have lost our way.
Baa! baa! baa!
We're little black sheep who have gone astray.
Baa! baa! baa!
Gentleman songsters off on a spree,
Doomed from here to eternity,
Lord have mercy on such as we.
Baa! baa! baa!

21. *COME HOME AGAIN TO WALES*

Far away a voice is calling, Bells of mem'ry chime
"Come home again, come home again" they call through the oceans of time.
We'll keep a welcome in the hillsides; we'll keep a welcome in the vales.
This land you knew will still be singing when you come home again to Wales.
This land of song will keep a welcome and with a love that never fails,
We'll kiss away each hour of Hiraeth when you come home again to Wales.

22. *THE WILD COLONIAL BOY*

There was a Wild Colonial Boy, Jack Duggan was his name,
He was born and bred in Ireland near a place called Castlemaine,
He was his father's only son, his mother's only joy,
And dearly did his parents love the Wild Colonial Boy.

At the early age of sixteen years he left his native home;
And to Australia's sunny land he was inclined to roam.
He robbed the rich and he helped the poor; he shot James McEvoy
A terror to Australia was the Wild Colonial Boy.

He loved the prairie and the bush where rangers rode along
With his gun stuck in his holster deep he sang a merry song.
But if a foe once crossed his track and sought him to destroy
He'd get sharp shooting sure from Jack the Wild Colonial Boy.

One morning on the prairie wild Jack Duggan rode along
Listening to a Mocking bird singing a cheerful song
Out jumped three troopers fierce and grim Kelly, Davis and Fitzroy,
They had set out to take and hold the Wild Colonial Boy.

"Surrender now! Jack Duggan, come! You see there's three to one!
Surrender in the Queen's name Sir! You are a plundering son!"
Jack drew two pistols from his side and glared upon Fitzroy,
"I'll fight but not surrender!" cried the Wild Colonial Boy.

He fired a shot at Kelly which brought him to the ground.
He fired point blank at Davis, too, who fell dead at the sound
But a bullet pierced his brave young heart from the pistol of Fitzroy;
And that was how they captured him the Wild Colonial Boy.

23. *WORRIED MAN BLUES*

It takes a worried man to sing a worried song
It takes a worried man to sing a worried song
It takes a worried man to sing a worried song
I'm worried now, I won't be worried long.

The train I ride is twenty-one coaches long
The girl I love is on that train and gone.

I went across the river and went to sleep
When I awoke I'd shackles on my feet.

Around my leg are twenty-one links of chain
And on each one initials of my name.

I said to the Judge, "What's gonna be my fate?"
"Twenty-one years a-working for the State!".

24. *ONE MORE RIVER*

Mr. Noah once he built an ark.
There's one more river to cross.
He patched it up with hickory bark
There's one more river to cross.

> One more river and that old river to Jordan
> One more river. There's one more river to cross.

The animals went in one by one
The elephant chewing a caraway bun.

Two by two: the bug, the flea and the kangaroo.

Three by three: the elephant trod on the bumble bee.

Four by four: the fat rhinocerous stuck in the door.

Five by five: some were almost more dead than alive.

Six by six: the monkey up to his usual tricks.

Seven by seven: said the ant to the hippo "Who the hell are you shovin'?"

Eight by eight: some had to hurry because they were late.

Nine by nine: Old Noah shouted "Heave that line!"

Ten by ten: if you want any more you can sing it again.

25. *FRANKIE AND JOHNNY*

Now Frankie and Johnny were lovers
Lordy, lordy how they could love.
They swore they'd be true to one another
Just as true as the skies above.
He was her man; he wouldn't do her wrong.

Frankie and Johnny went a-walking
Johnny had on a new suit.
Frankie went a-walking with Johnny
Thinking just how her man looked cute.
He was her man; he wouldn't do her wrong.

"Now listen to me darling!
I won't be very long.
Don't wait up for me lover
Don't worry while I am gone.
I am your man; I wouldn't do you wrong!"

Frankie went to the corner
To get her a bottle of beer.
She said to the old bartender man
"Has my loving man John been here?
He is my man; I think he's doing me wrong!"

"I don't want to cause no trouble
But I don't want to tell no lies.
Your loving man John was here just now
With that no-good Nelly Bligh.
There was your man. He was doing you wrong!"

Frankie looked over the transom
There to her great surprise.
Was her loving man John right over there
Making love to Nelly Bligh.
There was her man. He was doing her wrong.

Frankie pulled back her kimono
And she pulled out a big forty-four!
Rott-a-toot-toot! Three times she shot
Right through that hardwood door.
She shot her man who was doing her wrong.

The first time she shot him he staggered
The second time she shot he fell.
By the third time she pulled that trigger, Man
Her Johnny was burning in Hell.
He was her man but he was doing her wrong.

"Bring out your rubber tyred hearses!
Bring out the pony and trap!
I'm taking my lover to the graveyard, Man,
And I aint a-gonna bring him back.
He was my man but he did me wrong!"

Sheriff came round in the mornin'
Said it was all for the best.
Said that her lovin-man Johnny
Had been nothing but a goddam pest.
He was her man, but he'd done her wrong.

Frankie she said to the Sheriff
"What are you gonna do?"
Sheriff says, "Sorry Frankie gal
It's the 'Lectric Chair for you.
You shot your man, 'cause he'd done you wrong."

Last time I ever saw Frankie
She was frying in the 'Lectric Chair.
Sweat was a-pourin' down her brow
And the sparks was in her hair.
She'd shot her man, ' cause he was doing her wrong.

This story aint got no moral
This story aint got no end.
This story only goes to show
That there's no dam' good in men.
Just watch your man, he'll be doing you wrong.

26. *I WANT A BEER*

I want a beer just like the beer
That pickled dear old Dad.
It was a beer and the only beer
The Old Man ever had.
A real old fashioned beer with lots of foam
It took six cops to get the Old Man home.
So that's why I want a beer, just like the beer
That pickled dear old Dad.

27. *I AINT A-GONNA GRIEVE MY LORD*

A preacher went down to the celler to pray,
He prayed all night and he prayed all day.
A preacher went down to the celler to pray,
He prayed all night and he payed all day.
I aint a-gonna grieve my Lord no more
I aint a-gonna grieve my Lord
I aint a-gonna grieve my Lord
I aint a-gonna grieve my Lord no more.

Oh you'll never get to Heaven on a B.S.A.
'Cause Beeza bods don't ride that way.

You'll never get to Heaven on a Velocette
No Velo fellow's got there yet.

You'll never get to Heaven on a two-stroke Scott
For the noise it makes, the Lord likes not.

You'll never get to Heaven on a Matchless twin
For Matchless blokes are steeped in sin.

Oh you'll not get to Heaven on a Greeves I guess
For Scrambler's leave the place a mess.

Now you'll not get to Heaven on a Bog-wheel, Mate
'Cause you'll try to climb those pearly gates.

You won't get there on an Arrow two-stroke
You're a special friend of the other bloke.

You won't get to Heaven on a Norton Manx
The Lord don't want no race track — thanks!

You won't get to Heaven on a Fanny B
For the Lord's got shares in the Yank Harley.

You won't get to Heaven in a bubble-car
Nor a mo-ped they won't go that far.

You won't get to Heaven in a leather suit
The Lord thinks mods look far more cute.

If you want to get to Heaven, get a vintage bike
For the Lord admits they're what he likes.

Don't say you've been to the Dragon, Lad
For the Lord thinks that we're all stone mad.

For the Conway Club, there's just no hope
They've never learned the use of soap.

Join the Fifty-Nine, that's the thing to do
And the Reverend Bill will get you through.

BILL HUME

28. *THE MERRY MONTH OF MAY*

Upon her head she wears a silver skid lid
She wears it in the springtime and the merry month of May.
And if you ask her why the Hell she wears it
She'll say it's for a Ton-up who is far far away.

Now on her scooter she has got a sidecar
She's got it....

And in that chair she has three bonny triplets
She's got them....

Behind the door her father keeps a shotgun
He keeps it....

And now she sits and weeps upon a gravestone
She weeps there in the springtime and the merry month of May.
And if you ask her why the Hell she weeps there
She'll say its for a Ton-up who is six-feet down.

BILL HUME (*more or less*)

29. *PHIL THE FLUTER'S BALL*

Have you hears of Phil the fluter from the town of Ballymuck?
The times were going hard with him in fact the man was broke,
So he just sent out a notice to his neighbours one and all.
As how he'd like their company that evenin at a ball.
And when writing out he was careful to suggest to them
That if they found a hat of his convenient to the door
The more they put in whenever he requested them
The better would the music be for battering the floor

With a toot of the flute and the twiddle of fiddle O
Hopping in the middle like a herring on the griddle O.
Up, down, hands around, crossing to the wall
Oh hadn't we the gaiety at Phil the Fluter's Ball.

Mister Dennis Dougherty who kept the "Running Dog,"
There was little crooked Paddy from the Tiraloughett bog,
There was boys from every Barony and girls from every art
And the beautiful Miss Brady in a private Hoss and Cart
And along with them came bouncing Mrs. Cafferty
Little Mickie Mulligan was also to the fore
Rose, Suzanne and Margaret O'Rafferty
The flower of Ardmagullion and the Pride of Petravore.
With a toot....

Little Mickie Mulligan got up to show them how
And then the widow Cafferty steps out and makes her bow
"I could dance ye off your legs." say she "As sure as ye are born
If ye'll only make the piper play "The Hare was in the Corn"
So Phil plays up to the best of his ability
The ladies and the gentlemen begin to do their share
"Faith, then Mick, it's you that has agility"
"Begorra Mrs. Cafferty you're leaping like a hare".
With a toot....

Phil the fluter tipped a wink to little crooked Pat
"I think it's nearly time" says he "To pass around the hat"
So Paddy passed the caubeen round and looking mighty cute
Sez "Ye've got to pay the piper when he tootles on the flute!"
Then they all joined in with the greatest joviality
Covering the buckle and the shuffle and the cut
Jigs were danced of the very finest quality
But the widow beat the company at handelling the foot!
With a toot....

30. *HEN WLAD FY NHADAU.*

Oh land of my fathers how fair is thy fame
Entwined are proud memories about thy dear name
The lays of thy minstrels. Thy warriors renown
Give honour and grace to thy crown.
Wales! Wales! Sweet are thy hills and thy vales.
Thy speech and thy song! To thee they belong
Oh may they live ever in Wales.

No more on thy ramparts is heard through the night
The trumpet's loud summons to haste to the fight.
The contest is over yet proud my heart thrills
To gaze on thy victory crowned hills.
Wales! Wales! Sweet are thy hills and thy vales.
Thy speech and thy song! To thee they belong
Oh may they live ever in Wales.

31. *ALL THROUGH THE NIGHT*

Every star in heaven is singing.
All through the night.
Hear the glorious music ringing
All through the night.
Songs of sweet ethereal lightness
Wrought in realms of peace and brightness
See the dark give way to lightness.
All through the night.

Look my love the stars are smiling
All through the night.
Lighting smoothing and beguiling
Earth's sombre plight.
So when age brings grief and sorrow
From each other we can borrow
Faith in our sublime tomorrow
All through the night.

32. *AULD LANG SYNE*

Should auld aquaintance be forgot and never brought to min?
Should auld aquaintance be forgot and days of auld lang syne?
For auld lang syne my dear
For the sake of auld lang syne.
We'll tak a cup o' kindness yet for the sake of auld lang syne.

And here's a hand ma trusty friend and gi'es a hand o' thine
And we'll tak a richt guid willie waught for the sake o' auld lang syne.
For auld lang syne my dear
For the sake of auld lang syne.
We'll tak a cup o' kindness yet for the sake of auld lang syne.

33. *GOD SAVE THE QUEEN*

One last word — the contents are the responsibility of the Conway Club — cries of Shame! — not B.S.A.'s. On our heads be the burden of the guilt. Laurence Irving will point the finger at poor me anyway but I have got proof that I'm not to blame alone!
Ever thine,

BILL HUME,
(Dartmoor & Wormwood Scrubs, 1964.)

HAPPY
WEEK-END
TO ALL

DRAGON RALLYISTS

from BSA

B.S.A. Motor Cycles Ltd., Birmingham II

1548/65